# THE RAILWAYS OF
# PRESTON

## HALF A CENTURY OF CHANGE

# EUXTON, FARINGTON & PRESTON.

From Fleetwood
LEA ROAD

Fr. OXHEYS

To Longridge

2m 45c

Fr. Lancaster
36c

GREEN BANK SID.
30c

P. & W. GOODS (MAUDLANDS)
P. & W. GOODS BRCH JN

DEEPDALE PASS.
2.4c

33c

JUNCTION

11c

0m 68c

DEEPDALE GOODS

RIBBLE BRANCH
1m 23c

DOCK

P. & W. JUNC.
10c
19c

1m 30c

14c
P. & L. JUNC.

16c
Dock Street Jn.

PRESTON

STRAND ROAD JUNCTION
3.9c

JOINT PASS. & Jn.
(FISHERGATE)
24c

BUTLER STREET GOODS
(L. & Y.)

CHRISTIAN ROAD GOODS (L. & N.W.)
36c
W. LANCS. STA. GOODS

21c
JUNC.

25c

39c

0m

R. RIBBLE

RIBBLE JUNCTION
0m 26c
22c

30c

32c

1m 24c

PENWORTHAM JUNCTION
28c
23c
23c
28c

WHITEHOUSE JUNC.

MIDDLEFORTH JUNC.

From Southport

0m 74c

PRESTON Jn. STA.
JUNCTION

FARINGTON WEST JUNC.
8c

0m 57 1/2c

0m 58c

9c

0m 49c
JUNCTION

BAMBER BRIDGE STA.

To Blackburn

1m 0c

37c

23.7c
JUNC.

0m 46c

17c

30c

45c

BOSTOCK HALL STA.

EAST JUNC.

MOSS LANE JUNC.
55c
PASS.
20c

18c

GOODS JUNC.

FARINGTON

1m 60c

1m 33c

From Liverpool

MIDGE HALL

LEYLAND

1m 34c

EXPLANATION

| | |
|---|---|
| CORPORATION OF PRESTON | |
| LANCASHIRE & YORKSHIRE | |
| LONDON & NORTH WESTERN | |
| L. & Y. & L. & N.W. JOINT | NORTH UNION |
| | PRN & LONGRIDGE |
| | PRESTON & WYRE |
| N. UNION & CORPORATION JOINT | |

EUXTON

JUNCTION
12c
L. & Y. STA.

To Bolton

1m 24c

To Wigan

BALSHAW LANE & EUXTON

# THE RAILWAYS OF
# PRESTON
## HALF A CENTURY OF CHANGE

# ANDREW FOWLER

ATKINSON
PUBLICATIONS LTD

Cover illustrations:

Front cover (top): *A circa 1970 view of Preston's platforms 6 to 9 (today's 4 to 7), after the end of steam but prior to electrification.* **Martyn Hilbert.**

Front cover (bottom): *Steam in the preservation era: Stanier 'Jubilee' 5690* Leander *is sandwiched by more modern motive power at the north end of Preston station.* **Adrian Bradshaw.**

Back cover (top): *Stanier 'Black 5' 45345 stands outside Lostock Hall shed on 21 April 1968. Alongside, a pair of 8Fs await their fate following withdrawal.* **Peter Fitton.**

Back cover (bottom): *An unidentified Class 40 departs Preston with a southbound express on a sunny winter morning in the mid-1970s.* **Tom Sutch.**

Frontispiece: *A 1913 Railway Clearing House diagram of the arrangement of lines in the Preston area.*

Title page: *Caprotti valve gear fitted BR Standard Class 5 73129 accelerates away from Preston past Farington Curve Junction with an up parcels train on 20 September 1967.* **Peter Fitton.**

Published June 2012

Atkinson Publications Limited
PO Box 688,
Preston,
PR3 8AX
www.atkinsonspublications.co.uk

British Library Cataloguing in Publication Data.
A catalogue record for this book is available from the British Library.

ISBN 978 0 9565 1849 1

Typesetting and Origination by Andrew Fowler.
Printed and bound by CPI Group (UK) Ltd, Croydon, CR0 4YY

# Contents

# Acknowledgements

I would like to take the time to thank the following people for their kind assistance, without which the production of this book would not have been possible.

Firstly, my special thanks go to Adrian Bradshaw, who spent long hours restoring many of the images you will see in these pages, and who also introduced me to several of the photographers that have kindly allowed me to reproduce their excellent pictures.

I'd like to thank all those that have supplied me with images for this book: Bill Ashcroft, Ben Brooksbank, Martin Brown, Alan Castle, David Eaves, Dave Felton, Ron Fisher, David Ford, David Fowler, Tony Gillett, Arthur Haymes, Martyn Hilbert, Mick Langton, Trevor Machell, Jed McCormick, Bernard Mills, Arthur Nettleton, Martin Nield, Mike Norris, Peter Rigby, Alan Robinson, Paul Rose, Keith Sergeant, Ivan Stewart, Tom Sutch, Phil Tyrer and Tony Woof.

Of these, particular thanks go to Peter Fitton and Martyn Hilbert, both of whom have spent several hours trawling their collections to find exactly what was needed!

Finally, I must thank my wife Belinda for her patience and forebearance while I was preparing this book.

In memoriam: Matthew Banks and Helen Kitson.

# Foreword

Being born in the 1970s, I wasn't around before the end of steam on British Railways. I was a child of the BR 'Rail Blue' era, and remember blue and grey Mark 1 and Mark 2 coaches and various long-gone diesels and electrics vividly. The changes that the railways in the Preston area have undergone even since that time are significant; stations have come and gone, branches have been singled and semaphore signals have vanished.

Preston station has undergone yet more changes in recent times in connection with the introduction of the strengthened 11-car 'Pendolino' trains, with platforms 5 and 6 lengthened to accommodate them. Clearly, to have the Anglo-Scotttish expresses use the much longer and wider main island platform faces would be too sensible!

The station and surrounding lines, even those that have long since been closed, are continually evolving and there are regular calls to give the station, which has been described as 'dated' and one of the ten worst in its category, a facelift. With the chance that this could alter the station beyond all recognition, as with nearby Blackburn, and with Preston Guild year upon us once more I thought it was time that a book was produced charting the changes that the local railways have undergone since the mid-1950s.

Thanks to the photographers listed above, I was offered a massive selection of some 15,000 photographs to choose from. The hardest choice has alwas been which ones to leave out - with so many views of interest in my grasp, this book could easily have been twice the size! A number of the older images were a little 'soft', mainly due to the quality of the film that was available at the time; nonetheless several of these illustrated something unique, and so have been included.

What has resulted is certainly neither a definitive history nor a 'coffee table' book, but I hope it will evoke many memories for Prestonians young and old, and serve as a reminder of what 'Proud Preston' was really like in the days of our youth.

Andrew Fowler

June 2012

# PRESTON STATION (NORTH UNION SIDE)

**Above:** *Until the 1971 - 72 remodelling there were through lines and a horse dock to the west side of Preston Station. The location of this shot is betrayed by No. 2A signal box, which straddled the steep descent of the Ribble Branch to the dock. This can still be identified today by the gap in the parapet of the retaining wall.* 46228 Duchess of Rutland *shunts parcels vans at Preston on 29 May 1964. Now relegated to these duties, it was withdrawn less than five months later.* **Peter Fitton.**

**Previous page:** *The present station frontage dates from 1880 and has changed little since its construction, save for the demolition of the fine glass entrance canopy in the 1950s and its replacement with a more modern equivalent. This view shows the building and approach ramp leading from Fishergate in the 1960s.* **Paul Halton.**

## Background

Until 1972, what we now recognise as Preston railway station was only part of the story, and was referred to as the 'N.U. side'. This is because the first railway to arrive in the town (as it was then, only becoming a city in 2002) was the North Union Railway (NUR), which approached from the south in 1838. Its station was constructed more or less on the site of the current one, on the south side of Fishergate, originally as a terminus.

The Lancaster & Preston Junction Railway (LPJR) was the next on the scene, arriving in June 1840 and providing a route northwards out of Preston; however, it was not originally connected to the NUR system and had its own station, Maxwell House, to the north side of Fishergate. This situation was soon rectified by the NUR, which constructed a tunnel beneath the road and thus created a through route. However, it charged such heavy tolls for through trains that those from the north soon resumed calling at Maxwell House, with passengers walking between the two stations to continue their journey.

The Poulton & Wyre Railway (PWR) connected the Fylde area to Preston in July 1840, but again initially had its own station at Maudlands (almost directly below St Walburg's church). This was to the east of the line to Lancaster, which thus had to be crossed on the level by all trains from Poulton. This potentially dangerous situation was largely overcome in February 1844, when normal passenger trains began to use the NUR station; however, Maudlands station continued in use as a goods station until 1885, and was also regularly employed for excursion traffic.

**Above:** *This view of the through lines, taken from the erstwhile platform 1, shows 'Horwich Crab' 42783 passing by the horse dock with a container train on 3 August 1965. By this time the horse dock saw little use and would soon be swept away, along with the all the lines seen in this photograph.* **Tony Gillett.**

**Below:** *Seen from a similar vantage point a little further along platform 1, now-preserved Riddles BR 9F 2-10-0 92212 heads a train of 'presflo' cement wagons along the down through line. Note the signals located alongside the horse dock, and the length of its platform compared with the short section of corrugated iron canopy.* **Ben Brooksbank.**

You can almost feel the frost in the air as Fairburn 2-6-4T 42224 banks a northbound freight away from Preston on the through lines on the west side of the former platform 1 on 2 January 1967. The locomotive is just about to pass beneath Fishergate bridge, with some of the windows of County Hall visible through the exhaust. **Peter Fitton.**

**Above:** *One of Lostock Hall's Fairburn 2-6-4Ts, 42187, stands in platform 2 with the 19:10 to Wigan on a very wet 23 December 1965. The covered footbridge is just visible to the top left of the photograph, and the side screens added to the main station overall roof in the 1950s can be seen to the right.* **Peter Fitton.**

**Below:** *The original platforms 1 and 2, added on the west side of the station in 1903, were lengthened and converted for parcels use during the 1971 - 72 remodelling. In this 1979 view English Electric Type 4 (Class 40) 'Whistler' 40 026 stands in the former platform 2 with what appears to be a newspaper train; while most of the rake of vans consists of BR-designed vehicles, the fifth van from the front is of Southern Railway origin.* **Martyn Hilbert.**

Trains from Manchester and Bolton began to use the station from 1843 with the opening of the Bolton & Preston Railway (BPR); this line was originally planned to follow the route of the Lancaster Canal tramroad, but instead joined the NUR main line from Wigan at Euxton Junction, near Chorley. The line lasted a mere twelve months in BPR ownership before it was taken over by the aggressively-expanding NUR.

Next to arrive was the Preston & Blackburn Railway, which swept in from the east in 1846, originally joining the NUR line just south of the latter's Farrington (sic) station. However, the tolls levied by the NUR for the use of its metals between Farington and Preston were so high that the Preston & Blackburn eventually constructed its own route as detailed in the next chapter.

To cope with the additional traffic provided by all the new routes arriving in the town, the NUR's Preston station was progressively enlarged in a piecemeal fashion, and within a couple of decades was decidedly ramshackle in both appearance and overall condition. Part of the roof collapsed in 1866, but due to the number of companies involved in the running of the station, an agreement for its improvement took some time to be reached and work did not start until 1873.

## The present station develops

The first phase in the station's reconstruction involved the replacement of the narrow Fishergate tunnel by a wider bridge of girder construction, which paved the way for the widening of the site and the accommodation of more tracks. Work on the station itself began in 1877, and centred around the provision of a huge new island platform, booking office and buildings; work was completed in 1880. The main island was 1225 feet long and 110 feet wide, with a pair of bays provided at the south end. Two narrower island platforms were also built, one on either side, with an additional single-faced platform to the eastern side giving a total of seven faces available for through trains. The whole station was covered by an ornate iron and glass overall roof. Access to the station from Fishergate was via a cobbled approach ramp to the main building; the ramp then continued onto the north end of the main island platform itself, with footbridges leading off either side to the remaining platforms. A passenger subway also linked the platforms at the south end of the station, with a further separate subway for the movement of goods and luggage.

*In this view of the former platform 3, the arrangement of the run-round loops is apparent. Note the rather ugly footbridge covering, added in the early 1950s when the trainshed over the area between these two platforms was removed. Though the date is not known, the reporting number 1L23 chalked on the smokebox door of 'Black 5' 44769 identifies the train as the 13:20 Summer Saturday train from Crewe to Windermere.* **Ben Brooksbank.**

**Above:** *Riddles 7MT 'Britannia' class pacific 70023* Venus *lets off steam in platform 4 (now 2) at the head of a northbound express on 24 June 1964. While the maroon signs and parcels trolleys are a thing of the past, the station is still instantly recognisable. The yellow dustbins were some of the first 'corporate' era additions, but these would eventually be swept away in the wake of a number of bomb scares on the national network in the 1990s.* **Tony Gillett.**

**Below:** *Sulzer Type 2 (Class 25) 'Rat' 25 299 occupies a similar spot, albeit facing the opposite direction, in the same platform almost exactly 15 years later. The catenary has arrived, the platform is now renumbered platform 2, and the enamel signs have gone - but most other things remain the same. The train is a southbound track recording special, and the date is 26 June 1979.* **Bernard Mills.**

**Above:** *The Metro-Cammell (Class 101) DMUs were arguably the most successful of the first generation units, and lingered on in the Preston area until 2003. Here, a unit in Network SouthEast livery (a colour scheme rarely seen north of Birmingham until these units were displaced) departs the current platform 1 for Blackpool North. Visible to the left is the former platform 2, now extended and converted for parcels use.* **Martyn Hilbert.**

**Below:** *In contrast, the Metropolitan Vickers Type 2 Co-Bos (Class 28), whose design stemmed from the 1955 Modernisation Plan, were extremely unreliable locomotives. Following frequent failures soon after entering service in 1958, all 20 members of the class were banished to Barrow shed (12E) where their poor reliability was less likely to cause problems to other trains! They were fairly regular visitors to Preston in their latter years on the Manchester Victoria to Workington services; on 19 June 1963, class pioneer D5700 suffers the ignominy of being removed from one of these trains in platform 4 by 'Black 5' 45195.* **Peter Fitton.**

With just two companies – the Lancashire & Yorkshire and London & North Western railways – operating from Preston by the end of the 1880s, a much more harmonious existence ensued. So that through portions could be conveyed between the companies' trains, and also to allow multiple trains to use the long island platforms, a pair of crossovers was provided mid-way along the lines to the east of the main island platform. The two companies also collaborated to build a grand hotel to the south-east of the former North Union station. The Park Hotel was constructed in an ornate Gothic style, complete with tower, high on the hill above Avenham Park, allowing it to dominate the Preston skyline. The hotel was directly linked to the main island platform by a covered footbridge.

The station site was still constricted at the north end thanks to Charles Street, which lay immediately to the west of the station and was accessed off Fishergate. As a result, the route north was laid to a sharp curve between Fishergate bridge and the junction with the Poulton & Wyre line, and a 10mph speed limit was applied to this section. However, as speeds increased – particularly in the 1890s with the 'Race to the North' – this restriction became a significant problem. In 1896, an LNWR Scotch express derailed and was wrecked after taking the curve at an estimated 40mph; at this time, further measures were proposed to improve the station. Charles Street was demolished and the station cutting widened significantly; Fishergate bridge was lengthened in a westerly direction and a further island platform added. To the west of the new island platform line, a pair of through lines and a horse dock siding completed the improvements. Access to what had once been Charles Street goods yard and the horse landing was accomplished via Christian Road, which now bounded the extremity of the station. A further, somewhat shorter, iron and glass overall roof connected the original platforms with the new ones. The work was completed in 1903. Renumbering of the platforms consequently took place following the enlargements, with the through platforms numbered 1 to 9 from west to east. Under this sequence, the main island platform faces were numbered 5 and 6, with the two bays at the south end 5b and 6b. Despite being firmly located in the western side of the station, southbound trains on platforms 8 and 9 could only access the East Lancashire line, while those using platform 7 could use either route.

*Stanier 'Black 5' 45681 waits for the road at the north end of platform 5 (now 3) with a northbound freight on the foggy evening of 13 January 1961. The 'fire devil' beneath the water column has not been lit, so presumably frost is not expected - but judging by the cinders surrounding it the winter must have been a cold one!* **Tony Gillett.**

**Above:** *Lancashire might well have been the last stronghold of steam, but diesels were still relatively early interlopers to this part of the world. Later Derby Lightweight car M50963 is leading a formation of at least 5 cars, as it stands in platform 5 at 8:40pm on 30 December 1960. An indication of the immense parcels trade at the station can be seen around the train. At this time around 70, 000 parcels were handled each week.* **Tony Gillett.**

When British Railways took ownership of Preston station in 1948, the years had taken their toll. A lack of maintenance during the Second World War meant that the buildings, and in particular the glass and iron overall roof structure, were in appalling condition and on the verge of falling down. With much of the national network in a similar state, the £210,000 cost of repairing the whole station roof was beyond the reach of British Railways' pocket. In 1951, the decision was made to demolish part of the overall roof and replace it with canopies that did not stretch beyond the platform faces; however, work did not begin until 1955 and was finally completed in 1960. The glazed roof covering platforms 1 to 3 was removed entirely, and those over the remainder of the station were cut back significantly. After the elegance of the overall roof, the appearance of the modern steel canopies was stark by comparison. Their construction at Preston was the first instance of the 'gull wing' design on the West Coast Main Line, though they would feature at most of the principal stations on the route within the next decade. At the same time, the Park Hotel was closed, being taken over by Lancashire County Council for use as offices. The ornate gardens were partially converted into a car park for staff, with the remainder later providing the land for a hideous concrete office block that would mar the setting of the graceful hotel building and, ironically, house the council planning department!

Otherwise, the station arrangements remained the same for the rest of the decade. As the 1960s dawned, services began to be dieselised and, with the advent of the Beeching cuts, curtailed as routes were either closed or declined in status. With less trains now including through portions, far fewer were divided or combined at Preston. Passenger numbers were also dwindling; the western station was thus suffering from an over-provision of facilities and its condition was once again deteriorating. As a result, platforms 1 and 2 on the western side were officially closed to passengers from 1972 (though in practice they saw only occasional passenger trains from 1969) and used thereafter for parcels traffic.

**Lower right:** *An unidentified Class 50 enters platform 5 from the south with a down express on 22 May 1971. At this time the station was in the throes of remodelling, and this was the last full year before the catenary began to appear in the station. The array of trolleys on what was the principal northbound platform is vast, but all were needed as Preston handled around 70,000 parcels each day! Passenger traffic, on the other hand, seems sparse in this view.* **David Ford.**

**Above:** *The advent of elecrification is apparent in this shot in the form of the diagonal yellow stripe on the cabside of the locomotive, indicating that it was banned from the electrified network south of Crewe. Stanier 'Jubilee' 45654* Hood *lets off steam at the north end of platform 5 (now 3) on 4 April 1966.* Hood *had just two months to go before withdrawal, but was in good fettle beneath the dirt. Note the new style canopies at the platform ends, relics of the roof renewals. Just visible spanning the tracks beyond the passenger footbridge is another bridge, provided so that luggage could be sent to the platforms directly from the station approach; this was swept away during the remodelling.* **Tony Gillett.**

*The 'Royal Scot' was the most prestigious train on the LMS in its formative years and the name continued in use after nationalisation, being applied to the equivalent electric-hauled service (which was not so prestigious!) until 2003. Thankfully, with the arrival of the 'Pendolinos' the travesty of applying the title to a characterless multiple unit was avoided! For the train's Golden Jubilee in 1977, 87 003 was 'bulled up' with white wheel rims, silver buffers, gleaming paintwork and a headboard, in which condition it is seen at the north end of platform 3.* **Peter Fitton.**

## Remodelling

Electrification of the West Coast Main Line began in 1960 when the section from Manchester to Crewe was opened; the route from there to London was electrified in November 1965 with public services commencing in April 1966. Government approval for the extension of the scheme to Glasgow Central was given in 1970, and work to facilitate this started at Preston the following year. Also in 1970, the acceleration of West Coast Main Line passenger train services from London to Glasgow began, with electric locomotives replaced by double-headed Class 50s at Crewe, the latter type becoming a common sight at Preston.

Aside from the appearance of the catenary stanchions, the work brought massive changes to the station, which was extensively remodelled during the period 1971 - 72. With the closure of the old platforms 1 and 2, work began at this side of the station. The two through lines here were lifted, along with the track serving the horse dock, and the horse dock itself was demolished. The line through the erstwhile platform 1 remained in place to allow works trains to pass through the station without encumbering passenger traffic, though in time part of this was also dismantled, leaving a short bay at either end.

*This view of Preston station approach is pure nostalgia, and there are no excuses for including it! The mock-up Class 86 on top of the new canopy heralds the impending arrival of electric services from the station and the modern British Rail signs have appeared beneath it. Nonetheless, adorning the top of the main station building is an original maroon enamel sign! I wonder where that is now? There is a proliferation of British Motor Corporation products on the forecourt. **Peter Fitton.***

The resultant gap was filled with a road apron, which enhanced the platforms' new role as a parcels depot by creating a direct cross-platform rail to road interchange. Parcels trains of the 1970s were still lengthy affairs, and to cater for these the old platforms 1 and 2 were significantly extended at the south end, finishing beneath Fishergate bridge. In order to provide clearance for the forthcoming overhead wires, tracks were lowered beneath some structures. Such an attempt was made beneath the western end of Fishergate bridge, but this quickly proved abortive when a significant depth of soft ground or sliding sand was found immediately below the level of the existing ballast. As it proved both exceedingly difficult and prohibitively expensive to excavate to stable ground beneath the structure, this approach was quickly abandoned after the first few lines had been so treated. Instead, the existing rail level was maintained and the bridge deck raised on deeper girders.

While work was undertaken on the west side, trains were routed through the eastern side or via the East Lancashire line into the Butler Street side of the station. Track layouts were amended in a piecemeal fashion, with short sections on odd alignments connecting new with old, and severe speed restrictions in place through the station. Nonetheless, the train services continued, and a six-hour service between London and Glasgow was maintained on weekdays for most of the time during the reconstruction.

**Above:** *To the south end of the main island platform are two bays; in steam days they were referred to as platforms 5b and 6b. Stanier 'Jubilee' 45600* Bermuda *waits to depart with a local train on 6 March 1965. Above and behind the locomotive is the footbridge to the former Park Hotel, still in use for council employees at the time and a popular vantage point for spotters!* **Tony Gillett.**

**Below:** *Until the recent decline in parcels traffic, the bays were frequently used for such trains, or for the stabling of stock, at quiet periods. In this circa 1980 view, an unidentified Class 25 waits in platform 3c (originally 5b) while its train is loaded. A couple of restaurant cars are stabled in the adjacent bay.* **Keith Sergeant.**

*The extent of both bays is apparent in this early 1980s view, with a brace of Class 87s in original condition stabled between duties. These locomotives were supremely reliable, and were the mainstay of West Coast Main Line services through Preston for three decades before being ousted by the Pendolinos. Visible above and to the left of 87 024* Lord of the Isles *is the parcels conveyor leading to the Royal Mail parcels depot.* **Keith Sergeant.**

By mid-March 1972, the works to the west of the station were nearing completion, and the whole of the East Lancashire side was closed. The remaining platforms continued in use and were renumbered. Platforms 3 to 8 became the new platforms 1 to 6 in order; the erstwhile platform 9 was also retained; however as it was never intended to be used by passenger trains, no number was originally displayed. The curves linking the west side of the station with the East Lancashire side were lifted and buffer stops installed to make the future platforms 6 and 7 a pair of temporary bays for the duration of the works. Afterwards, the lines from the south side of these platforms were realigned to meet the new gentler West Coast Main Line approaches. Similarly, in anticipation of the arrival and passing of 110mph expresses, the south ends of platforms 3 and 4 were also reconstructed on a new alignment, with the ramps lying approximately four yards west of their previous position. The old alignment can still be traced today, as one of the canopies constructed in the 1950s provides a guide to the original course of today's platform 3.

Many familiar station structures disappeared or were changed beyond recognition during the remodelling. The familiar maroon and cream BR London Midland Region colours, including the enamel signs, were swept away, along with the station signalboxes (see Chapter 11), and the lattice structure of the footbridge was boxed in to guard against the chance of stray luggage – or even limbs – coming into contact with the overhead lines. By 1972, trains with through portions were a thing of the past, so the crossovers between platforms 4 and 5 were removed. The lengthy main island platforms (now 3 and 4) still allowed multiple trains to call at the same time, so each were numbered in two halves – as 3a and 3b for northbound trains or 4a and 4b for southbound ones. Correspondingly, the bay platforms at the south end were numbered 3c and 4c. While the majority of the platform faces remained more or less on the same alignment that they had occupied for the preceding 90 years, the station approaches changed beyond all recognition.

At the same time, the stanchions and portal frame gantries for the catenary swept through the station, though the system was not energised for a further twelve months, with the first electric passenger train from Preston to London running on 23 July 1973. Along with the introduction of the electric trains came other changes to 'modernise and improve' facilities at the station. These included the closure of the old station buffet and its replacement with Travellers Fare, complete with fast food, disposable cups and instant coffee.

**Above:** *Celebrated parallel-boilered 'Patriot' 45545* Home Guard *stands at the north end of platform 6 (now 4) at the head of a Manchester to Windermere train on 17 August 1962. This Preston-based locomotive would be the last unrebuilt member of the class to work a passenger train -* after *it had been officially withdrawn!* **Peter Fitton.**

**Below:** *The new order at Preston as English Electric Type 4s (Class 40s) D335 and D226 stand in platform 6 on 6 June 1961, having arrived with an express. While they were the most powerful diesel locomotives in the country at the time of their construction, they were no match for a 'Duchess' on top form and it was not unusual for them to double-head heavy trains, particularly over Shap. Visible to the right here is No. 3 signal box.* **Tony Gillett.**

**Above:** *Until the recent arrival of the Pendolinos, EMUs were very infrequent visitors to Preston. One service they did appear on in the late 1970s and early 1980s was the Summer Saturdays-only working from Crewe. A train formed of a pair of 4-car Class 304 units awaits departure from platform 4. Notice the long lattice section of the overall roof above and behind the front of the unit; this was required to support the structure above the lines that branched off at this point to connect to the East Lancashire side of the station.* **Alan Robinson.**

Electrification north of the station continued, with the first Anglo-Scottish services running on 6 May 1974. The following day, Queen Elizabeth II unveiled a plaque on one of the catenary stanchions on platform 4 commemorating the completion of the all-electric West Coast Main Line. With the new electric services came new rolling stock; a fleet of air-conditioned Mark 3 coaches (and Mark 2e and 2f vehicles supplementing them) was introduced, setting a new standard in passenger capacity (though certainly not in comfort!). To haul them, 35 Class 87s entered service between 1973 and 1975; along with the 100 members of Class 86 that were introduced from 1965 they were deemed to be suitable for providing the modern image British Rail wished to portray, finally banishing the last relics of the steam age from the north west. The older designs of electric locomotive – classes 81 to 85 – were normally relegated to secondary and parcels trains, and in particular classes 82, 83 and 84 were infrequent visitors to Preston. The arrival of the 'Electric Age' was celebrated with the installation of a large wooden mock-up of an electric locomotive on top of the canopy at the station entrance, though thankfully this embellishment was short-lived!

The station has changed very little in the last three decades, but thankfully some of its principal features have been restored in recent times. The overall roof has been cleaned and re-glazed, and the former luggage subway has now been fitted with new lifts and opened for use by passengers with limited mobility. With some peculiar reasoning that the author cannot comprehend, many of the Preston – London and Glasgow trains now depart from the narrow and featureless platforms 5 and 6, with the much wider and better-appointed platforms 3 and 4 utilised by local services that are not so well patronised. As a result, work has recently been carried out to lengthen platforms 5 and 6 to cater for the forthcoming 11-car Pendolino trains.

The former platform 9 has now finally been officially declared platform 7, though this is not normally used for service trains. Instead, the many summer charter trains frequently use it, and a convenient water standpipe makes it a popular layover point for the steam locomotives active today on the main line. However, its future may be in doubt as plans are afoot to remove it and widen the existing platforms 5 and 6 to provide better accommodation for Pendolino passengers. Only time will tell if this comes to pass!

**Above:** *The unique Riddles 8P pacific 71000* Duke of Gloucester *had a very short working life in British Railways ownership. Built in April 1954, its Caprotti valve gear was not particularly successful and it was withdrawn around a year after this shot, showing the locomotive in platform 7 (now 5), was taken on 6 June 1961. Thankfully 71000 was preserved and can be seen on the main line once more. The line in the foreground connected the main station to the East Lancashire extension route to Bamber Bridge and Lostock Hall.*

**Below:** *Ex-LMS 2P 4-4-0 40646 pauses in platform 7 with a train for Birmingham on 1 July 1961. The locomotive was based at Bescot shed (21B) at the time, from where it was withdrawn just under a year after this shot was taken. The period advertising adds colour to an otherwise bland scene.* **Both: Tony Gillett.**

**Above:** *Wasted power! Stanier 'Jubilee' 45571* South Africa *enters the north end of platform 7 with the 12:40 Blackpool Central to Manchester Victoria on 27 February 1963. Visible at the right-hand end of Fishergate bridge is the hydraulic accumulator tower for the station's lifts.* **Peter Fitton.**

**Below:** *By the time the early AC electrics made it to Preston 'under the wires' they were already in their twilight years and largely confined to parcels and empty coaching stock workings thanks to declining reliability. On a sunny summer day in the late 1970s, 85 017 and 84 003 purr through platform 5 past the site of No. 3 signal box with a train of bogie vans. The use of train reporting numbers has been abolished, with the headcodes displaying four zeros until the aperture could be blanked off.* **Alan Robinson.**

**Above:** *Following the Grayrigg accident in February 2007 which resulted in the writing-off of Pendolino unit 390 033, Virgin trains was left with a shortage of rolling stock. As an interim measure, a locomotive-hauled rake of coaches returned to regular use on the West Coast Main Line, with the necessary motive power provided by a Class 90 leased from either DB Schenker (formerly EWS) or Freightliner. EWS-liveried 90 029* The Institute of Civil Engineers *stands in platform 5 shortly after arriving with 1P05, the first of the Fridays only evening services from Euston on 14 August 2009.*

**Below:** *Coupled to 90 029 is the rake of Mark 3 coaches and Driving Van Trailer hired to complete the necessary train. These were repainted to match the livery applied to the Pendolinos, complete with grey and white shading over the doors, and the ensemble was subsequently dubbed the 'Pretendolino' by enthusiasts!* **Both: Martin Brown.**

**Above:** *At the south end of platform 7 (now 5), the West Coast Main Line skirted the edge of the East Lancashire station yard. Stanier 'Black 5' 45046 has, judging by its gleaming coat of unlined black, just been outshopped following a visit to Horwich works. The locomotive is standing beneath the footbridge to the Park Hotel, while the attention being received suggests that the cylinder drain cocks are giving cause for concern. The date is 12 May 1965.* **Tony Gillett.**

**Below:** *A brace of English Electric Type 1s (Class 20s), 20 084 and 20 086, pass through the station with a permanent way train on 23 May 1986 and are pictured in more or less the same spot as 45046 above. In the two decades between the images, the East Lancs. side of the station has been obliterated and the new Fishergate Centre, visible behind and above the rear locomotive, is nearing completion.* **Martin Brown.**

**Above:** *On very rare occasions, electric stock did pass through the station before the wires arrived. One of these took place on 21 December 1962 when Riddles 'Austerity' 2-8-0 90367 returned 'AM1' prototype AC EMU set 19 to the Lancaster - Morecambe - Heysham branch following overhaul. These three-car sets were converted from old fourth-rail stock in 1952 in order to test the then new AC catenary system, but even the new Multiple Unit Green livery could not disguise the dated origins of the wooden-bodied stock, which would last until 1966. Driving Motor Brake Second Open car M28129M is leading as the train trundles through the platform 8 (now 6) road.* **Tony Gillett.**

**Below:** *Stanier 'Black 5s' survived in the Preston area until the very end of steam, and were equally at home on secondary express services and local passenger trains. 45394 waits in platform 8 with the 16:22 to Wigan on 11 July 1964.* **Peter Fitton.**

**Above:** *An English Electric Type 4 (Class 40) gets away from platform 6 with a parcels train in the late 1970s. The train is comprised of a mix of 4-wheel and bogie vans, including an ex-Southern Railway utility van; these vehicles lingered on into the early 1980s.* **Keith Sergeant.**

**Below:** *The age of the train: an Inter-City APT-P formation with unit 370 006 at the rear pauses in platform 6 on 4 August 1980. While the APT was ultimately unsuccessful, its technology lives on in today's Pendolinos. This view gives a good impression of the station between the remodelling and the arrival of the Fishergate shopping centre. The top of the Butler Street station entrance is visible to the left, above the short tunnel that once led to platform 13.* **Dave Felton.**

**Above:** *At the time this view was recorded in October 1966, platform 9 (now 7) was firmly in the East Lancashire side of Preston station; this shot of Stanier 'Jubilee' 45627* Sierra Leone *waiting with a southbound train therefore leads us neatly towards the next chapter. Unlike the station to the west of this point, almost everything has changed since this shot was taken; gone are the ornate canopies visible through the arches, and passenger trains rarely call at this platform.* **Tony Gillett.**

**Below:** *Standing in a similar position to* Sierra Leone *in the above photograph, but facing the opposite way, is preserved 'Black 5' 45231. During the summer at least one steam train a week still calls at the station, and platform 7 is a regular layover and watering stop for the locomotives. While the platform road today connects with the erstwhile North Union line, its origins are clear to see as the platform itself still curves away towards the former East Lancashire Railway route.* **Author.**

# PRESTON STATION (EAST LANCS. SIDE)

**Above:** *The vantage point here is in front of the Park Hotel, and the view shows the yard at the East Lancashire side of the station. The Stanier 'Princess Coronation' (or 'Duchess') beneath the overall roof is standing in platform 6 (now 4), while the line next to it leads from platform 7 (now 5). The lines of the former East Lancashire Railway route to Bamber Bridge emerge from beneath the short overall roof before sweeping sharply off to the right. The date is 9 May 1964.* **Peter Fitton.**

**Previous page:** *The Cravens-built DMUs were quite handsome machines, and were popular with passengers on the Accrington - Blackburn - Preston route on which they were first introduced in the north west in the early 1960s. A two-car power twin set is depicted here in platform 11 bay; in the background, No. 3 signal box is undergoing demolition, dating the view to May or June 1972.* **Jed McCormick.**

When it first began operating to Preston in 1846 after amalgamation with the Blackburn & Preston Railway, the East Lancashire Railway (ELR) initially worked its trains over the North Union Railway's track from a junction at Farington; it also used the latter company's main station at Fishergate. However high tolls and congestion prompted the ELR to construct its Preston extension from Bamber Bridge junction in 1850 (see Chapter 7), although despite this fact its trains continued to share the increasingly dilapidated NUR platforms. As discussed in the previous chapter, conditions in the station at the time were cramped and overcrowded, and when the new station was opened in 1880 the Lancashire & Yorkshire Railway (LYR) – which had absorbed the ELR some 21 years previously – shared one platform with the NUR (the current platform 5) and had another two on the east side dedicated for its sole use (now numbered platforms 6 and 7). In addition, two south-facing bays were provided to the east of the main station.

Goods traffic was, as with all early railways, an important commodity and a large single-storey warehouse was constructed in 1850 to cater for it. Also provided were a small carriage shed, engine shed and turntable for its locomotives. Once in the LYR's tenure the goods facilities greatly improved, culminating in 1884 with the provision of a huge 5-storey warehouse, which was accessible by road via Butler Street and through an underpass beneath Fishergate. This incredible building remained in situ until the mid-1980s with the lettering 'LANCASHIRE AND YORKSHIRE RAILWAY GOODS WAREHOUSE' clearly visible in white paint on its slate roof right up to the time of its demolition.

**Lower right:** *Another of the distinctive Cravens (Class 105) sets has arrived in platform 8 via the East Lancashire Railway's Preston Extension route with a terminating service and disgorged its meagre cargo of passengers in this circa 1970 view. The picture shows a wealth of detail on platform 9; the doors on the left of the picture lead into the buildings constructed by the LYR in 1913.* **Martyn Hilbert.**

**Above:** *Looking south from the end of the short trainshed on the East Lancashire side of the station, the sharp curve to take the lines beneath Vicars Bridge can clearly be seen in this atmospheric shot. Stanier 'Black 5' 44926 waits to depart with the 12:25 Blackpool to Liverpool on 3 January 1964. The silhouette of the Park Hotel dominates the skyline.* **Peter Fitton.**

**Above:** *A last look at the south end of platform 9 (now 7), with the unique Stephenson Link Motion-fitted 'Black 5' 44767 standing alongside the water column while a platelayer attends to a track defect in the platform 8 road. Just visible through the archway to the right of the picure is part of the ironwork suporting the canopy on platform 11. Platform 9 ended immediately forward of the locomotive, after which point a short bay - platfom 10 - existed. 44767 was completed at Crewe works by the LMS on the last day of that company's existence, 31 December 1947. This historic locomotive has thankfully been preserved,* **Tony Gillett.**

In 1913, the LYR embarked on a period of further improvements to the station when it added its own entrance and a small range of buildings directly to the east of the main station. These were accessed off Butler Street, and contained a booking office with two ticket windows, waiting rooms, parcels offices and provision for a station master; until LMS days the two sides of the station were looked after by the individual operating companies. At the same time, an additional bay platform and through platform were added, the line to the latter passing beneath the new station buildings.

The buildings themselves, though small in comparison to those on the main station, were attractively styled with a facade in the late Art Nouveau fashion of the period, with big decorative arched windows and a wrought iron and glass canopy over the main entrance. The eastern side of the building faced directly onto the goods yard approach ramp, and both this aspect and the rear were somewhat plain with only small window apertures. Nonetheless, decorative balustrades extended round all three open sides of the building, the fourth side being made up by the eastern wall of the main station.

In the 1950s, the East Lancashire side of the station was extremely busy. It consisted of platforms 8 – 13, of which 10, 11 and 12 were all south-facing bays. Platforms 8 and 9 (today's platforms 6 and 7) were through platforms beneath the shortest section of overall roof, and the tracks feeding these were connected to the West Coast Main Line at the north end of the station. To the south, the lines then passed beneath Vicars Bridge, east of the Park Hotel, by means of a set of sharp S-curves.

Platform 10 was a short bay built on the end of platform 9 which was capable of handling a five-coach train, while platforms 11 and 12 were considerably longer; all curved to the east along their length. An ornate wrought iron and timber canopy covered the length of platforms 10 and 11, but in contrast platform 12 was completely unprotected from the Lancashire weather! Platform 13 occupied the most easterly position of all, squeezed in between the walls supporting the main station overall roof and the approach ramp for Butler Street goods yard.

**Above:** *Had you walked through the archway visible in the previous view, you would have emerged here, on the forecourt of the East Lancashire bay platforms. To the right is platform 10, with a Class 108 idling away in the bay, while a Mark 1 coach is stabled at the buffer stops of platform 11.* **Martyn Hilbert.**

**Below:** *Walking to the left of the previous vantage point (and travelling back in time about a decade!) you would be rewarded with this view. To the left is the through line serving platform 13, while the coaching stock is stabled in platform 12 bay. The canopy protecting bay platforms 10 and 11 is visible above the train, with the Park Hotel towering above the scene. The chimneys of the vicarage that gave its name to Vicars Bridge can be seen at the far left of the picture.* **Colin Reid.**

**Above:** *Looking the other way from the old fish dock platform in 1976 following closure of the East Lancs. extension line, the substantial cantilever canopy that once covered platform 13 can be seen. The area once occupied by the track has been filled in, but the LYR station buildings still stand. However, all traces of these have since been completely swept away.*

**Below:** *The station buildings provided in 1913 by the LYR were accessed via Butler Street, with parcels loading bays along the side which were reached from the ramp to the goods yard. Behind the wall to the left is the canopy structure on platform 13, indicating the point at which through trains emerged from beneath the building.* **Both: Paul Rose.**

**Above:** *The LYR building facade was constructed in an ornate, late Art Nouveau style, complete with balustrading around the top and a canopy over the entrance doors. The latter had long gone by the time of this 1983 view, but the places on the wall previously occupied by the brackets can clearly be seen. Less than two years after this photo was taken, the building was demolished and no traces now remain.* **Martin Brown.**

**Below:** *Leaving platfom 9 behind, Stanier 'Jubilee' 45627* Sierra Leone *departs Preston via the East Lancashire exit in October 1966 with a train for Liverpool. Platform 10, with its ornate curved canopy, is on the left with the East Lancashire Railway goods warehouse beyond. This view clearly shows the sharply-curved exit from the main station towards Vicars Bridge, which is visible in the distance.* **Tony Gillett.**

**Above:** *Unrebuilt and un-named Fowler 'Patriot' 45517 stands in platform 11 with a Liverpool train on 5 March 1962, while Stanier 2-6-4T 42475 simmers gently alongside in platform 12 as it awaits departure with a Southport-bound working. The 'Patriot' was based at Bank Hall, Liverpool, at the time and was a frequent visitor; however it was withdrawn three months after this photo was taken and scrapped at Crewe works that July.* **Tony Gillett.**

Access to these platforms was via an internal staircase from the LYR main entrance that led into the small platform-level buildings between platforms 9 and 13, though passengers could also walk across through the archways at the south end of platform 9.

Trains for Accrington, Blackburn and Liverpool were the most frequent users of these platforms, with Southport services supplementing them. During the summer, however, the station saw a vast increase in traffic during the so-called 'wakes weeks' when, in the 1950s and early 1960s, most of the mills and factories in towns of Lancashire and Yorkshire would shut down for either one or two weeks and the workforce would head for a seaside holiday by train. Literally dozens of extra trains were laid on from Accrington, Rochdale, Colne, Blackburn and Leeds to the resorts of Blackpool, Morecambe and Southport, with almost all of them travelling via the East Lancashire side of Preston.

In addition, the vast majority of express trains travelling from the north to Blackpool would pass through this side of the station. While this might sound odd, it was a common occurrence for these trains to pass through the East Lancashire side of the station, run via the Preston Extension line to Lostock Hall and then loop round at Farington to return northwards, stopping to pick up or set down in the North Union side platforms. This rather complicated sounding arrangement was actually very simple, and avoided the need for a locomotive swap in order to change direction. Thus, 'Duchesses' and other top link motive power regularly appeared in what was otherwise a part of the station that dealt with secondary trains.

DMUs were frequently seen in the East Lancashire platforms from the early 1960s; a fleet of Cravens units (which later became Class 105s) was allocated to Accrington shed, thus becoming known as 'Accrington sets' to crews and spotters alike. The Southport trains, however, remained steam-hauled to the end with the line becoming an early victim of the so-called 'Beeching axe' in September 1964 (see Chapter 9). Despite tank locomotives being the normal motive power for such trains, most engines were detached and turned at Preston.

**Above:** *There's an absolute wealth of detail in the scene depicted here; most of the East Lancashire side of Preston is visible, including part of the original East Lancashire Railway goods shed of 1850. Caprotti valve geared 'Black 5' 44729 is waiting to depart platform 10 with the 17:29 to Southport on 3 September 1964.* **Peter Fitton.**

**Below:** *'Jubilee' 45627 Sierra Leone again, in pre-yellow cabside stripe days this time, standing in platform 11 bay with a Liverpool train on 22 May 1962. The locomotive was based at Bank Hall, Liverpool, amd was a regular visitor to Preston. Alongside, in platform 12, Lostock Hall-based Stanier 2-6-4T 42546 awaits departure for Southport.* **Tony Gillett.**

**Above:** *LMS 3-cylinder compound 4P 4-4-0 41186 waits to depart platform 12 with a Southport train in October 1957. These locomotives were fairly infrequent visitors to Preston by this time, though the outwardly-similar 2P locomotives appeared quite often in the mid-1950s. The sharp curvature of the lines meant that a check rail was necessary to help prevent derailments. The water column appears to be receiving some attention - note the ladder and the absence of the canvas 'bag'.* **Arthur Nettleton.**

Goods traffic added significantly to train movements at Butler Street, with the railway's goods warehouses fully employed into the mid-1960s. Fruit and vegetable produce from the fertile West Lancashire growing district was brought in on a daily basis, together with such variable traffic as day-old chicks (around 400 boxes of these a week were forwarded from Preston in the mid-1950s) and carrier pigeons, along with calves and sheep on market days. Fish traffic was of major importance too, with a dedicated dock opposite platform 13 on which most of the local market stallholders had a shed. In addition, the postal and parcels traffic was concentrated here; around 70,000 parcels and two and a half million letters were handled each week in the late 1950s, which were despatched via the luggage subways to the platforms for onward travel. Those sorted on the station for delivery in the Preston district were transferred to road vehicles - which in the 1950s included vans, horse-drawn wagons and Scammell Mechanical Horses - via loading bays in the side of the LYR Butler Street building. This work started at around half past three in the morning and continued until seven at night.

As the 1970s dawned, passenger traffic on railways throughout Britain was declining sharply and Preston was no exception. Between road competition and the Beeching cuts much of the feeder traffic for both passengers and goods on local routes had gone. With modernisation of the West Coast Main Line under way, a re-evaluation of the way the station was run saw the East Lancashire side earmarked for closure in 1972. However, it was allowed one last busy period before demolition. Remodelling of the station began on the western side, with the lines for platforms 1 to 5 lifted for realigning in stages. While this work was going on, most trains used the East Lancashire platforms, with many travelling via the Preston Extension line to Lostock Hall (see Chapter 9) and rejoining the West Coast Main Line at Farington Junction.

By May 1972 this work had been completed, and this spelled the end for the East Lancashire platforms. Initially, the through lines in platforms 8 and 9 (now 6 and 7) were severed and provided with buffer stops, becoming in effect a pair of north-facing bays. The rails beyond were lifted with just the connecting line from platform 7 (now 5) remaining, allowing engineers' trains to use the Preston Extension and thereby avoid congestion on the other half of the station.

By this time the goods traffic had all but disappeared, and the still substantial parcels and mail traffic was concentrated on the other side of the station on the new purpose-built platforms (formerly 1 and 2).

**Above:** *One of the rare occasions on which a pacific type locomotive enjoyed a foray along the West Lancashire line to Southport took place on 23 May 1964 when Riddles BR 6MT 72007* Clan Mackenzie *was put in charge of a Railway Correspondence and Travel Society special. The train is pictured in platform 13, surrounded by spotters. Imagine trying to venture so far down a platform ramp today! The view was taken from the south end of platforms 10 and 11.* **Alan Castle.**

**Below:** *Taken from the same vantage point but looking straight along platforms 10 and 11 afforded this view. On a wet day in 1971, a pair of Cravens (Class 105) DMUs idle away, awaiting their departure time. The unit on the left (in platform 10) is for Colne. Visible behind the DMU on the right are the southernmost of the East Lancashire buildings including the cantilever canopy over platform 13, complete with maroon enamel signs directing passengers to the other platforms.* **Peter Rigby.**

**Above:** *A wonderfully evocative scene here, showing the crew of Southport shed based Fairburn 2-6-4T 42132 enjoying a cigarette break before departing platform 10 with the last train of the day to West Lancashire, the 22:39 all stations to Southport Chapel Street, in December 1963. The silhouette of Vicars Bridge and the lights of Preston East Lancs Goods box are visible beyond the platform end.* **Alan Castle.**

**Below:** *The Preston Extension of the East Lancashire Railway entered the station environs under Vicars Bridge, which provided access to the Park Hotel on East Cliff. Brand new English Electric 350hp shunter (Class 08) D4140 (which later became 08 910) has just been outshopped from nearby Horwich works, but has suffered an electrical problem during running in and failed while entering the station, partially blocking the yard. It is seen receiving urgent attention from a couple of fitters beneath the bridge on 13 August 1962.* **Tony Gillett.**

**Above:** *The East Lancs side of Preston was vast; from the popular spotter's vantage point of Vicars Bridge there was always something of interest to be seen, as is the case in this early 1960s view. A 'Black 5' brings a passenger train away from platform 13 while a pair of Cravens (class 113 with the distinctive large headcode box on the cab roof dome) DMUs are stabled in the yard. A number of parcels vans and covered wagons surround the former ELR goods shed.* **Phil Tyrer.**

**Below:** *Viewed from the same bridge but a little further along, this circa 1970 shot clearly shows platforms 10 (with a Class 108 DMU waiting) to 13 and the former ELR goods shed building; No. 3 signal box can also be seen in the upper left corner. Traffic is clearly tailing off and within a couple of years all the platforms visible here would close.* **Peter Rigby.**

*Looking slightly to the right from the same vantage point as the previous view, the huge goods warehouse provided by the Lancashire & Yorkshire Railway can be seen, and despite being around 85 years old is still in good condition and well-cared for. However, despite the deceptive presence of a large rake of ventilated vans in the foreground, freight traffic is in terminal decline in the wake of the Beeching cuts and increasing competition from road transport. To the left of the warehouse the tunnel beneath Fishergate, by which road vehicles could enter the goods yard, can be seen. This survives today as an access point to the Fishergate Centre car park.* **Peter Rigby.**

The carriage sidings between the station and the foot of East Cliff were very rapidly torn up, though the goods sidings were seen as less of a priority and were gradually dismantled over a period of a couple of years. Platforms 10 to 13 suffered a similar lingering demise, remaining in situ for some time after the track that once served them had been lifted. Eventually they were stripped of their fixtures and fittings and the gaps between them filled in, though the large canopy cantilevered over platform 13 survived until the mid-1980s. Butler Street goods yard, including the aforementioned platform areas, became a car park for staff and passengers, though its origins were clear to see as the original cobblestones and platform paving slabs were not surfaced over.

After the remodelling, platforms 7 (which was shared by trains using both East Lancs. and North Union lines), 8 and 9 survived, albeit with the track realigned and routed through the area once occupied by the carriage sidings in order to link up with the West Coast Main Line. The south end of platforms 7 and 8 were extended along the new formation and became the new platforms 5 and 6. Only the southern tip of platform 7 betrays its origins today, still curving away towards the east while the track heads due south.

The end finally came for the two goods warehouses in 1984 when the whole area was cleared to make way for the massive and uninspiring Fishergate Shopping Centre development, with much of the site becoming an enormous car park accessed via the former goods yard ramp at Butler Street. The road access tunnel to the former goods yard also remains, providing shoppers with a means of reaching the car park from Charnley Street without needing to cross the busy Fishergate thoroughfare.

The LYR station buildings succumbed to the wrecker's ball in 1985, and every trace of these fine structures was obliterated. The area once occupied by the buildings was filled in to make a ramp for a taxi rank, with a bland modern canopy erected to provide only the barest protection from the elements; the current station entrance from Butler Street takes the primitive form of a hole in the wall. The one-time existence of platform 13 is belied by the surviving entrance to the tunnel that once passed beneath the buildings, which is visible next to the north end of platform 7. All other traces of the route to Vicars Bridge have all but vanished following the erection of a multi-storey car park on the site of the bay platforms and sidings.

**Above:** *Around a decade and a half after the previous view, on 5 September 1984, the warehouse is in appalling condition and demolition is under way. The space previously occupied by lines of wagons is now a parking place for passengers' vehicles, almost all of which could be considered classics today!*

**Below:** *On the same date, the former East Lancashire Railway goods shed is also undergoing demolition. It's a shame that these two historic and imposing strucures have not survived to give an insight into the importance of Preston's goods traffic; the sites for both are now beneath the immense Fishergate Centre car park.* **Both: Martin Brown.**

**Above:** *This shot shows the track rationalisation west of the former platform 1 in the winter of 1971. The horse dock and through lines have been removed. The line of the former platform 1 remains in situ to provide access to the north and south ends of the station for the works trains. Eventually this line would be cut and this area paved to provide the road apron for the parcel concentration depot and these days forms part of Network Rail's Preston site.*

**Below:** *The date is 1971 and here we can see the civil engineering works starting just north of Fishergate bridge. Part of Pitt Street Sidings and the through lines have been removed and the slow lines are now disconnected (where the red banner is located). Meanwhile the railway continues to operate, and all services are using the fast lines and East Lancs. side of the station. This is typical of the project with piecemeal alterations being made as the work progresses.*

**Above:** *It's 1972 and the new goods line and platform 6 are taking shape. The lines in the foreground were the former platform 8 and 9 roads; currently these are stopped off to provide a pair of temporary bays. The East Lancs. side of the station is now out of use for passenger services but is retained for the engineers' trains. Preston No.3 signal box, which closed on 13 March 1972, can be seen in the centre of the picture.*

**Below:** *A Class 104 DMU passes beneath Fishergate bridge on the line serving the former platform 4, now 2. The modifications to the structre are clearly visible; this work was to provide the necessary clearance for the overhead traction wires. A new foot was added to the existing girder beams and the original foot then removed. In the background can be seen the brand new parcel platform, extending to the far side of the bridge.* **All: Bill Ashcroft;** © **Mike Norris.**

*This 2002 aerial view of Preston shows the extent of the land that was once occupied by the station and its environs. The ent[ire]
area now covered by the Fishergate Centre and its car park was, until 1972, taken up by the East Lancashire side of the stat[ion]
and Butler Street goods yard. The area to the left is occupied by the Royal Mail sorting office and was once Christian R[oad]
goods yard. The dock branch can be seen curving sharply past this site, while at the top of the picture the junction where [the]
Blackpool line branches off to the west can be discerned.* **Ian Hammond.**

**Above:** *In May 1972, Class 50 402 is departing south from the current platform 4 (former platform 6). No. 3 signal box has completely disappeared by this time and the new line serving platform 6 has been laid, together with the goods loop. A new colour light gantry has been rected, ready for when Preston Power Box takes over in nine months' time. A support for the overhead catenary can be seen to the right.* **David Ford.**

**Below:** *With the overhead wiring finally completed, electric haulage of public services finally commenced north of Preston in May 1974. On May 7, a special shortened formation of the Royal Train took to the West Coast Main Line behind a spruced-up Class 87 87018, with test coach 'Mentor' - used to check the overhead line equipment - included at the front of the train, along with an air-conditioned Mk 2 vehicle. The newly-extended parcels platform is to the right of the locomotive.* **Tom Sutch**

# THE APPROACH FROM THE SOUTH

**Above:** *The site of the original Balshaw Lane & Euxton station, which was closed in 1969, is once again in use by local trains. It took nigh on 30 years for the new Euxton Balshaw Lane platforms to rise from the ashes and they are a poor substitute for the original. The present station is no more than a rudimentary halt with the now-common 'bus stop' style waiting shelters. 'Sprinter' unit 156 490 departs southwards on a Liverpool Lime Street working.* **Martin Brown.**

**Previous page:** *On a cold and crisp 2 January 1967, Riddles 9F 2-10-0 92218 passes Ribble Sidings, just south of the River Ribble, with an up freight. Visible above the train to the left of the shot is the Park Hotel, while to the right of the locomotive is one of the high-rise flats that are now known as Sandown Court; both of these structures can be used to place the view today.* **Peter Fitton.**

As mentioned in Chapter 1, today's West Coast Main Line had its origins in the North Union Railway (NUR). This company itself was formed from the first amalgamation of railway companies in Britain, namely the Wigan Branch Railway (which was opened in 1832 to connect collieries in the Wigan area to Parkside on the Liverpool & Manchester Railway) and the Wigan & Preston Railway. The latter company was incorporated as early as 1831, but was unable to raise enough capital to begin construction until the formation of the NUR in 1834. Train services to Preston finally commenced on 31 October 1838. The NUR line was leased jointly to the Grand Junction and Manchester & Leeds railways; these companies subsequently went on to become part of the London & North Western and Lancashire & Yorkshire Railways respectively. The NUR was eventually formally taken over by these two companies in 1889 and, until the LYR was finally absorbed by the LNWR the year before the Grouping, formed the only jointly-owned section on the whole of the West Coast Main Line between London and Carlisle.

We begin our northward journey to Preston at the village of Euxton near Chorley, which today has a population of just over 8,000. Its small size does not preclude an interesting railway history, with no less than four stations and a busy junction being located here over the years. The first station was provided adjacent to the Bay Horse Inn on what is today Euxton Lane when the NUR opened. This was closed in 1895 when a replacement station called Balshaw Lane and Euxton was provided three-quarters of a mile to the south, where the fast and slow lines separate slightly to the east and west respectively. In the 1950s this had two platforms located on the slow lines; these were equipped with timber buildings and were then served principally by stopping trains to Wigan. Like most staffed stations in the area at the time it had goods facilities, but these were formally withdrawn on 8 March 1965.

**Above:** *We divert off the main line for a short distance onto the original Bolton - Preston route to share this rare shot of the original Royal Ordnance Factory station at Euxton near Chorley, which shows rebuilt 'Patriot' 45531 Sir Frederick Harrison waiting for passengers at shift change time on 27 May 1964. The station was considered fairly basic in its day, with very plain steel and concrete canopies, but it looks positively palatial by modern standards!* **Tony Gillett.**

**Below:** *A unique passenger's eye view of one of the R.O.F. platforms, with Stanier 'Jubilee' 45584 North West Frontier waiting to depart with a train for Preston on 19 May 1964. One of the 20-foot high walls securing the perimiter of the explosives factory can be glimpsed through the portal of Central Road (now Central Avenue) overbridge.* **Tony Gillett.**

**Above:** *Today, a brand new Buckshaw Parkway station stands on the site of the former R.O.F. Halt. The new facility opened in October 2011 to serve Buckshaw Village and the business parks that have sprung up on the adjacent land. The original halt, though closed in 1965, was left almost intact for nearly four decades, finally being demolished in 2002. This view depicts 'Adelante' unit 180 103 waiting to depart with a service to Hazel Grove on 28 October 2011.* **Martyn Hilbert.**

**Below:** *Leaving the West Coast Main Line behind, rebuilt 'Royal Scot' 46168* The Girl Guide *rounds the curve from Euxton Junction with a Manchester train on 11 April 1962. To the right can be seen some of the massive array of sidings used by the Royal Ordnance Factory in its heyday; though only a handful of wagons are visible here the site was still exceedingly busy at this time.* **Tony Gillett.**

*Ivatt 4MT 'Flying Pig' 2-6-0 43046 and Riddles 'BR5' 4-6-0 73039 stand side-by-side in the sidings at the Royal Ordnance Factory, Euxton, on 13 July 1967. Both locomotives are in deplorable external condition and both would be out of traffic for good by the end of the year. First to go was 73039, withdrawn from Patricroft MPD that September, while Lostock Hall shed's 43046 was officially out of service from 25 November.* **Tony Gillett.**

In line with the recommendations in Beeching's report, 'The Reshaping of Britain's Railways', the station was closed altogether from 6 October 1969 and subsequently flattened. Along with many of the closures resulting from the 'Beeching axe' the removal of Balshaw Lane station proved to be short-sighted and, following pressure from the public and the County Council, a new station was constructed on the site of the original. Euxton Balshaw Lane, as it is now called, opened in 1998 and takes the form of a basic unstaffed halt with rudimentary 'bus shelter' passenger accommodation that makes the original LNWR station of 1895 look palatial by comparison!

The other two stations in the area were located on the Bolton & Preston Railway (BPR), which opened in June 1843 to meet the NUR at Euxton Junction, approximately two-thirds of a mile north of the latter company's original station by the Bay Horse Inn. The BPR provided its own Euxton station (later called Euxton Junction to avoid confusion with the station on the West Coast Main Line) on the curve to the east of the junction; this was a simple affair, which is perhaps unsurprising owing to the distinctly rural nature of the area at the time. Traffic was sparse enough to justify its closure by the Lancashire & Yorkshire Railway, firstly on a temporary basis from 2 April 1917 and officially from 12 April 1920.

The Royal Ordnance Factory opened what was to become the largest armaments plant in Britain at Euxton in 1938 on a site immediately south east of Euxton Junction. Known as R.O.F. Chorley, it employed around 28,000 people at the height of World War II, principally on shell-filling duties but was also the location where the bouncing bombs, designed by Barnes Wallis for the 'Dambusters' raids, were manufactured. To enable the vast workforce to commute to and from the site, a railway station was provided, opening on 7 February 1938; originally known as Chorley R.O.F. Platform it was re-named Chorley Halt by May 1942 in an attempt to disguise its purpose. It was re-named R.O.F. Halt following the cessation of hostilities and was last used on 27 September 1965, though it survived almost intact beneath ever-encroaching undergrowth until 2002 when it was finally demolished.

In the interests of secrecy and safety public service trains did not call at the station; instead, dedicated trains were laid on, with a ticket window in the East Lancashire booking hall at Preston staffed specifically for the purpose. Trains to the site ran from Blackpool and Manchester, calling at some but not all intermediate stations. Unsurprisingly, the Royal Ordnance Factory generated significant freight traffic and a fan of sidings was provided, stretching between Euxton Junction and the site's railway station. These remained in use until the 1970s when the remaining traffic switched to road haulage.

**Above:** *This scene at Euxton Coal Sidings shows the shape of things to come in more ways than one. English Electric Type 4 (later Class 40) D341 charges southwards with an express on 22 April 1962. Meanwhile, in the background a crane is busy on the new M6 motorway works - the bridge over the railway has only just been installed.* ***Tony Gillett.***

**Below:** *Almost half a century later, and steam is once again in action at this location. In this shot taken from the other side of the line, Euxton Coal Sidings and the signal box have long gone, but the motorway bridge can just be glimpsed through the overgrowth at the very left-hand side of the picture. On the evening of 8 June 2011, new-build A1 60163 Tornado passes by the site during its loaded test run, following a period out of traffic for repairs.* ***Author.***

*Heading northwards from Euxton, we are now on the outskirts of Leyland as Stanier 'Jubilee' 45617* Mauritius *sweeps by on 17 June 1962, having just passed under Bent Bridge. The locomotive had just been transferred from Crewe South shed (5B) to Crewe North (5A), which presumably explains the absence of a shed plate on the lower part of the smokebox door! The train is entirely made up of LMS stock, though almost all of this would disappear over the next half dozen years.* **Tony Gillett.**

The R.O.F. site was gradually de-commissioned from the mid-1990s and fully closed in 2007. It has since been almost totally cleared to provide space for the new Buckshaw Village and Matrix and Euxton business park developments, and a new station to serve these has now been erected on the site of the former halt. Known as Buckshaw Parkway it opened on 3 October 2011 and, unlike the original station, is staffed during operating hours.

The section of the West Coast Main Line from Balshaw Lane to Euxton Junction is four tracks wide even today, with the slow lines paired together on the western side. The main line between Preston and Euxton Junction was quadrupled by the LNWR as early as 1880. The junction itself is north-facing only; today, as in steam days, the double-track main line from Bolton and Manchester merges onto the fast lines. However, the present arrangement is a much simpler layout to that used until the 1970s. Originally, trains from Manchester were able to pass directly to the down fast line, crossing the up fast line by means of a diamond crossing; those needing to pass to the slow lines in order to call at intermediate stations then passed over the up slow line in a similar manner. With the current junction layout, trains have to 'ladder' from one line to the next in order to traverse to or from the slow lines in either direction. While this is theoretically a more versatile arrangement, it reduces capacity and can create a bottleneck on the West Coast Main Line at busy periods. In steam days, a freight loop known as Euxton Coal Sidings was in use immediately north of the junction, controlled by a signal box of the same name that also acted as a block post on the main line.

One and a half miles to the north of Euxton Junction stands Leyland station. Opened in October 1838 by the NUR as Golden Hill (the station lies at the eastern end of Golden Hill Lane in the town), it was given its present name later that same year. Access to the station is from the road overbridge located at the north end of the platforms, though a separate footbridge is provided for cross-platform interchange. The station's current layout was formed in 1880 when the track was quadrupled, at which time the bridge and connecting Station Brow were constructed in order to remove the level crossing. Unlike Balshaw Lane, the station has four platform faces, with all surviving at the present time; however, stopping services are normally concentrated on the slow lines as there are no longer any long-distance trains that call at Leyland.

**Above:** *From the same vantage point as the previous shot, but this time looking north, the foot crossing between Hargreaves Avenue and Lynton Avenue can be seen. It is apparent that this is a favourite location for young spotters, including those depicted here watching in awe as 'Black 5' 45224 on the Up Fast line overtakes classmate 45337 (now preserved) which is on the slow line, having just re-started from Leyland.* **Tony Gillett.**

**Below:** *The chimney of Bashall's Mill in the background identifies this as almost the same location shown above, with pioneer Class 50 D400 (later 50 050) heading south with a test train on 20 September 1967. Just behind the train is the footbridge that has by now replaced the foot crossing, leading to the end of Lynton Avenue.* **Peter Fitton.**

*Stanier 'Jubilee' 45563* Australia *speeds downhill through Leyland station on the down fast line with an express passenger working on 22 April 1965. The locomotive was shedded at Warrington (8B) at the time, and was withdrawn that November. Note the concrete lamp standards and BR 'sausage' totem signs; all would soon be gone as Leyland's fortunes declined in the last years of the decade.* **Tony Gillett.**

Originally the westernmost platform contained the main buildings, including the original station master's house; the remaining platforms were equipped with the typical LNWR wooden waiting shelters. The main booking hall is located at street level adjacent to the west side of the road overbridge. Today, the latter is the only structure to survive, with the now-common rudimentary 'bus shelters' offering passengers meagre protection from the weather.

A large goods yard was laid out just to the north of the station, on the opposite side of the Station Brow overbridge and on the west side of the line. No less than eleven sidings were provided, together with a brick-built goods shed, offices and coal staithes. Parts of it lingered on in use until the mid-1980s, but it has now inevitably been flattened and the site covered with housing.

Continuing towards Preston, immediately north of Leyland station on the west side of the line lay the famous concern of Leyland Motors, manufacturer of lorries, buses, trolleybuses, tanks and diesel multiple units among many other diverse vehicles over the years. The site opened in 1914, and in the inter-war period a number of sidings were provided for the works. These continued to generate traffic for the railway until the 1980s, although as most readers will know the site suffered a downturn from the mid-1980s onwards and the company, which had seen several changes of identity over the years, was sold off to become Leyland DAF in 1987. Since that time, production has continued on the same site but has been significantly scaled back and the rail connection has recently been removed. The resident works shunter at the site from 1955 was a John Fowler 0-4-0 diesel, works number 4210108, which has since been preserved by the fledgling Poulton & Wyre Railway Society now based on the former Fleetwood branch.

On the opposite side of the railway from the Leyland Motors site lay Bashalls sidings, so-called because they were provided to serve the Mill Lane, Farington, factory of Messrs. Bashall and Boardman. The points of access to both this site and Leyland Motors sidings were controlled by Bashalls Sidings signal box, which was situated on the western side of the line.

Around three-quarters of a mile further north lies the south-facing Farington Junction, where the former East Lancashire Railway meets the main line adjacent to Fowler Lane overbridge. Until the remodelling of the 1970s, a number of sidings were laid out here to the east of the main line and it was common for locomotives working in from Yorkshire and the east coast to be exchanged for native London Midland Region ones at this point; ex-War Department Riddles 2-8-0s were a common sight here until 1966. Further coal sidings were laid out to the west of the line.

**Above:** *On a bright and sunny 1 May 1986 a Birmingham Railway Carriage & Wagon (Class 104) 3-Car DMU set pauses in platform 4 at Leyland with a Blackpool North to Manchester Victoria Service. This was a familiar time-honoured scene, the class 104s dominating these services during the the 1970s and 1980s until ousted by Cross-Country (Class 120) units.*

**Below:** *Class 81 (originally AL1) 81 007 arrives at Leyland with an early morning Birmingham International to Lancaster all-stations service on 18 June 1987. This was the only loco-hauled train to call at the station in recent times, and has since been discontinued. It left Leyland at 8am, mopping up a large number of Preston-bound commuters in the process.*

**Above:** *In the early 1980s a batch of Swindon built Class 120 Cross Country DMU sets were allocated to Newton Heath Depot, primarily for use on Manchester to Blackpool North services. M53680 brings up the rear of a Manchester Victoria to Blackpool North Service at Leyland on 9 November 1986. This part of Leyland station (on the down slow line) still had its low height platform, a legacy from the opening of the North Union Railway in 1838.*

**Below:** *Almost brand new and not yet in traffic, Class 150/2 Sprinter 150 219, with minimal yellow warning paint on its cab end, calls at Leyland on 12 March 1987 while on a crew training run between Blackpool North and Manchester Victoria. These units are still in use and can regularly be seen at Leyland.* **All: Martyn Hilbert**

**Above:** *Another brief stint of EMU operation in the area took place in the late 1980s in the form of a Saturdays-only working from Crewe to Preston. BR Wolverton Class 304 unit 304 039 bowls along the Up Fast at Farington just south of Leyland with the service from Preston to Crewe on 31 March 1988. The unit is passing the Leyland Motors Farington Works.*

**Below:** *The resident diesel shunter at Leyland Motors' Farington factory was a John Fowler 0-4-0, works number 4210108, built in 1955. The loco is seen outside the engine test shop in April 1982; the sidings shown here run parallel to the West Coast Main Line. After a long period out of use, the shunter has now been preserved.* **Both: Martyn Hilbert**

*Just a little further north than Leyland Motors but still in Farington, Stanier 'Black 5' 44927 of Blackpool North shed (24E) storms up the climb towards Euxton Junction with 1A35, the 12:25 Saturdays only Blackpool Central - Euston on 6 July 1963. Visible in the distance is the chimney of Bashalls Mill, now demolished and part of today's Farington Business Park. The signals here protect Farington Junction, which is just behind the train.* **Peter Fitton.**

Continuing north, the site of the original Blackburn & Preston Railway junction with the North Union line, abandoned by the ELR in 1850, could be discerned in steam days but today has been obliterated by housing. Immediately after passing beneath Croston Road bridge, trains reached Farington station. This was one of the original North Union stations dating from 1838, originally mis-spelled Farrington until 1857. Like Leyland it had a four platform layout, upgraded at the time of the 1878 – 1880 quadrupling; again a road level ticket office was provided though this was a small and simple affair. Timber waiting shelters in the typical LNWR style were installed on the platforms. However, throughout the BR era the meagre train services did little to encourage custom. No long-distance trains called there, and the presence of the nearby Lostock Hall station with its more frequent services to Preston only sped up its decline. Farington station closed on 7 March 1960 and was demolished soon afterwards.

Another three-quarters of a mile to the north lies Farington Curve Junction, where northbound trains from East Lancashire and Liverpool joined the West Coast Main Line (or where southbound ones for these destinations diverged). The signal box, which survived until 1972, sat in the shadow of Bee Lane overbridge and was squeezed between the fast and slow lines with the operating floor overhanging the running lines on either side. The signalman in charge of the 30 levers here was kept exceedingly busy, as the 'box controlled not only the junction with the slow lines but also the junction of the East Lancashire and Liverpool lines, which was situated immediately to the south west.

Only a few hundred yards to the north was Skew Bridge signal box, where a pair of through lines that took traffic on the avoiding lines through Preston commenced. Thereafter, the six tracks ran in parallel for the last mile to Preston station. After Skew Bridge, the line crossed Factory Lane where the large concern of Vernon's Surgical Dressings was situated from 1915 until as recently as 2006. Continuing north the line crosses the site of the West Lancashire route to Southport, closed in 1964 but still clearly discernable as a footpath today. Beyond this bridge lay Ribble Sidings, which were situated to the west of the main line. Four sidings and a shunting line and neck were located here, which along with the up and down fast, slow and through lines made for an impressive track layout! The sidings ended immediately south of the River Ribble, where the shunting line effectively became the start of the Ribble Branch to Preston dock.

A total of seven tracks crossed the Ribble bridge in the 1950s, with five on the stone-built five-arch viaduct that was widened in 1880 and a further pair on an iron lattice structure that was added on the west side as part of the 1903 station improvements. All but one of these lines remains in use today, the redundant one being the westernmost track on the iron viaduct spans. From here, until 1972 trains passed No. 1 and No. 1A signal boxes, opposite each other on the east and west sides of the line respectively, to enter the Preston station environs.

**Above:** *Dieselisation of the principal West Coast Main Line expresses is well under way in this view dating from 30 May 1964, as a brace of English Electric Type 4s (later Class 40s) D232 and D326 head north with the 'Royal Scot'. As an interesting aside, D326 was the locomotive involved in the August 1963 Great Train Robbery.* **Peter Fitton.**

**Below:** *This is almost a signalman's view, taken from ground level in front of Farington Junction signalbox; note the array of point rodding in the foreground. Riddles 9F 92016 hauls a freight train from the fan of sidings at the northern end of the junction in August 1967. This locomotive was based at Carnforth at the time, but was withdrawn just two months after this picture was taken.* **Tony Gillett.**

**Above:** *There is a wealth of detail in the second of our views of pioneer Class 50 D400 passing through Farington Junction from the Lostock Hall direction on its way from the Settle - Carlisle line with a test train on 20 September 1967. Steam is still very much in evidence - an 8F is just visible to the left of the picture, and the coaling plant of Lostock Hall MPD can clearly be seen on the skyline to the left of the bulk of Cuerden Green Mills, along with part of Lostock Hall gasworks.* **Peter Fitton.**

**Below:** *During the 1990s, the exchange sidings at Farington Junction were regularly used by Settle - Carlisle steam specials to change motive power. Here, Class 86 86254* William Webb Ellis *heads its train round the curve onto the main line, having just taken over the Southbound Cumbrian Mountain Express from Riddles 7MT 70000* Britannia *in August 1992 for the return journey to London Euston.* **Martyn Hilbert.**

**Above:** *Despite the last lingering vestiges of the steam age the BR corporate blue is making headway in this August 1967 view of Stanier 'Black 5' 44711 storming by Farington Curve Junction. The semaphores have gone, replaced by colour light signals, though these are still controlled locally from the junction signalbox, just visible behind Bee Lane bridge.* **Tony Gillett.**

**Below:** *Despite being taken only a handful of years before the previous picture, this shot of Riddles BR 2MT 2-6-0 78044 passing Farington Curve Junction signalbox on 22 July 1961 with a Liverpool - Preston working looks very dated in comparison. The train is comprised of LMS wooden-bodied non-corridor stock, and semaphore signals are in abundance.* **Peter Fitton.**

**Above:** *In this mid-1980s view from Bee Lane bridge, Class 87 Bo-Bo 87 033* Thane of Fife *passes Farington Curve junction on the down fast line. The houses to the left are located on Leyland Road. The locomotive in this view worked on the West Coast Main Line from 1974 until 2005, when it was exported to Bulgaria for further use.* **Martyn Hilbert.**

**Below:** *The pointwork on the slow lines at Farington Curve Junction was renewed in 2009, and the current formation is depicted in this view looking south from Bee Lane overbridge as an unidentified 'Pendolino' unit grinds through on a service to London Euston.* **Author.**

*This truly superb shot depicts Riddles 'Britannia' 7MT 70045 (originally* Lord Rowallan *but by now devoid of nameplates) heading south with a mixed freight on the up slow line between Skew Bridge and Bee Lane on 6 September 1967, as an unidentified 'Black 5' drifts tender first towards Preston. Note the board for the 15mph speed restriction through the junction, visible next to the front of the locomotive, and the semaphore signal post on which a colour light signal with 'feather' route indicators has been fitted.* **Peter Fitton.**

*This series of four images were captured at the popular trainspotting location of Skew Bridge in the Penwortham Lane area.* **Above:** *Rebuilt 'Royal Scot' class 4-6-0 46123 Royal Irish Fusiliers passes beneath the bridge, heading for Preston with a down parcels train on 1 August 1962.*

**Below:** *Shiny new English Electric 350hp (Class 08) diesel shunter D4142 (later 08 912) enters the goods loop with a trip freight working on 25 August 1962.*

**Above:** *On the same day as the previous view, Brush Type 2 (later Class 31) A1A-A1A D5832 (31 299) passes the signalbox with the 08:00 Sheffield to Blackpool North service. The locomotive was only a few months old at the time, and would last in traffic until 1990.*

**Below:** *A brace of Class 50s, led by 436 (the 'D' prefix having been dropped by this time), pass the signalbox on the slow line with a northbound express. The presence of catenary and semaphore signals together date this view to the winter of 1972/73.*
***All: Peter Fitton***

**Above:** *A last view of Skew Bridge signalbox in its last winter of operation, with a rare sighting of Gloucester Railway Carriage & Wagon Company (later Class 128) single car parcels DMU M55988 heading for Preston. These units were among the most powerful constructed at the time, with two 230hp Leyland Albion bus engines fitted. This allowed them to tow up to two BR bogie parcels vans.*

**Below:** *A pair of Metro-Vick Type 2 (later Class 28, though none survived long enough to be numbered as such) Co-Bos, with D5719 piloting, pass Factory Lane heading for Manchester woth a train from Whitehaven.* **Both: Peter Fitton.**

**Above:** *In a similar spot to the Metro-Vicks on the previous page, Brush Type 4 (Class 47) 47 110 hauls a Speedlink service past Factory Lane on 22 June 1987. In the foreground are the pair of goods loops which commenced at Skew Bridge, while one of the pair of gas holders from the former Lostock Hall gasworks can be seen to the left of the locomotive.* **Martyn Hilbert.**

**Below:** *In the 1960s, Ribble Sidings occupied part of the embankment between Factory Lane and the River Ribble viaduct. Waiting to depart from the goods loops here with a train of ICI hoppers from Burn Naze near Fleetwood on 24 March 1961 is unrebuilt Fowler 'Patriot' 45501 St. Dunstans.* **Tony Gillett.**

**Above:** *Stanier 'Black 5' 4-6-0 45145 leaves the Ribble viaduct behind and passes the entrance to Ribble Sidings on the evening of 4 September 1964 in charge of the 17:10 Blackpool North to Manchester Victora. The 1903 - 1904 iron lattice bridge extension is visible on the extreme left of the picture.* **Peter Fitton.**

**Below:** *English Electric Type 3 (Class 37) Co-Co 37 682 crosses the Ribble viaduct with 6L62, the 1215 Basford Hall to Salford Crescent ballast on 9 September 2001, having just run round its train in the station. When this photograph was taken on 6 September 2001 the locomotive was operated by the Englissh Welsh & Scottish Railway company. It survives today in the ownership of Direct Rail Services and can still be seen in the area working nuclear flask trains.* **Mick Langton**

**Above:** *A fine view of the southern approach to Preston station on 21 March 1961, with rebuilt 'Royal Scot' 46166* London Rifle Brigade *making a spirited departure southwards past the Park Hotel with a prcels train. No. 1 signalbox can be seen behind the vans, with the footbridge and covered walkway to the hotel partly visible.* **Tony Gillett.**

**Below:** *Brand new Brush Type 4 D1623 (later renumbered 47 042 in 1974, 47 586 in 1983 and 47 676 in 1991) passes No. 1 signalbox at the head of a 15-coach test train to Penrith on 29 September 1964; it officially entered traffic three days later. Judging by the escaping steam, the train heating boiler must be working. No. 1A signalbox can be seen behind the locomotive, next to the water tower. 47 676 was stored from 1994 and was cut up at CF Booth & Co., Rotherham, in 1998.* **Peter Fitton.**

**Above:** *Regional Railways-liveried Metro-Cammell 3-car DMU, 101 683, enters Preston station from the south with the 09.45 Manchester Piccadilly to Blackpool North Service on 12 April 1997. The Ribble viaduct can be seen in the background.* **Martyn Hilbert**

**Below:** *The day the Electric Age began in Preston. In a view that virtually captions itself, 87 002 departs Preston with the very first electric-hauled service to London Euston on 23 July 1973. A crowd of people can be seen on the south end of platform 3.* **Peter Fitton.**

# LINES TO THE NORTH

**Above:** *Judging by the 'feathering' of the safety valves, the fireman of Stanier 'Black 5' 45448 has things well in hand on departure from Preston, and is leaning from the cab ready to assist the driver with the sighting of signals. The train is 1Z65, a Blackpool Illuminations special, and is seen passing County Hall immediately north of Fishergate bridge on 8 September 1962.* **Ben Brooksbank.**

**Previous page:** *Unrebuilt and un-named Fowler 'Patriot' 4-6-0 45542 pilots Stanier 'Jubilee' 45700* Amethyst *away from Preston with a northbound express on 14 April 1961. The 'Patriot' appears to be putting in an absolutely incredible performance judging by the colour and amount of the exhaust! These locomotives were star performers even in original condition, and it is sad that none were preserved. Thanks to the LMS-Patriot Project, however, this scene could yet take place in perservation with new-build 45551* The Unknown Warrior *leading the way.* **Tony Gillett.**

Departing Preston in the northbound direction along the West Coast Main Line, trains passed beneath the impressive bridge carrying Fishergate and almost immediately ran alongside No. 4 signalbox, which was provided by the LNWR in 1902 during the enlargement of the station. Despite having only two storeys (the other major 'boxes in the area had three) in order to give the signalmen a view beneath the bridge, this was the largest such structure in the area, being 104 feet long, 12 feet wide and having 173 working levers. These controlled the northern approaches to the station, together with the line to the former canal basin, now filled in and known as Dock Street sidings; these were situated to the east of the line at this point. Later, this area became known as Ladywell House sidings after the new British Rail offices that were built on the site of the former basin. It was a regular stabling point for locomotives into the 1990s, but today sees only occasional use for engineers' stock. Ladywell House itself was demolished in the mid-1990s to make way for the new extension to the Ringway dual carriageway through the town.

The various exits from Preston merged together after passing either side of No. 4 'box, from which point on there were effectively six through lines. This arrangement reached and crossed Marsh Lane by means of a viaduct (today there is an additional bridge across the aforementioned Ringway extension), at the northern end of which stood No. 5 signalbox. The operating floor was 16 feet above rail level, though it looked considerably taller when viewed from the road below! A total of 126 levers were needed to work the complicated junction at Maudlands where four lines branched off westwards to Blackpool and the Fylde, diverged to the north and Lancaster while the Longridge line curved away to the east. Until September 1961, Preston's Motive Power Depot stood opposite No. 5 'box on the western side of the line. The shed here was mostly destroyed by a fire in June 1960 and survived for its final months as a roofless shell; in its latter days it was used as a storage area for withdrawn locomotives. Today the site is home to Preston Power Box, which controls the main line from Springs Branch near Wigan in the south to Burton in Kendal, around ten miles south of Oxenholme, to the north.

**Above:** *Looking north through the portal of Fishergate bridge, the sheer scale of the impressive gantry controlled by Nos. 4 and 5 signalboxes is evident as an unidentified 'Black 5' heads north with a fitted freight on a sunny day in March 1965. County Hall is just visible at the left-hand side of the picture, with No. 4 signalbox to the right. The line leading to the bottom of the picture serves platform 5 (today's platform 3) while that disappearing to the right leads to the short bay at the north end of the same platform.* **Tony Gillett.**

**Below:** *This view was taken at the north end of Preston No. 4 signalbox, and shows the complicated arrangement at the station throat. Stanier 'Princess Coronation' 46234 Duchess of Abercorn drifts towards the station with a southbound express, while an unidentified 'Black 5' waits for the road in the distance with a working from the Fylde on 9 February 1961.* **Tony Gillett.**

*Riddles 'Britannia' 7MT 70012 John of Gaunt starts away from Preston on 28 August 1964 with the 16:03 Manchester Victoria to Barrow-in-Furness working. The train is pictured passing No. 5 signalbox, which controlled the junctions with the Fylde and Longridge lines as well as the West Coast Main Line. County Hall and Fishergate Baptist Church are visible on the skyline in the background.* **Peter Fitton.**

**Above:** *A true 'driver's eye view' of the line north of Preston, taken from the footplate of a Riddles Standard Class 2 tank in 1964. Visible to the left are the remains of the Motive Power Depot with its LMS-built coaling tower, and Bretherton's corn mill, with St Walburge's church directly ahead of the locomotive and No. 5 signalbox to the right. Just to the north of the MPD, the line to Blackpool branches off to the left and the West Coast Main Line curves right.*

**Below:** *Slightly further north, Stanier 'Black 5' 45371 passes the site of the now-closed Preston Motive Power Depot with a down fitted freight on 15 May 1964. Some of the lamp columns in the shed yard are visible to the far right of the picture, while the roof of No. 5 signalbox can be seen above the first and second wagons.* **Both: Peter Fitton.**

*This view was taken from the opposite side of the line to the previous picture, and a couple of decades later. On a sunny day in 1985, Class 47 47 401 Great Eastern hauls a failed DMU set - a hybrid unit comprised of cars from Classes 108 and 101 - past newly-introduced 'Pacer' railbus 142 035. The Class 47 was the first of the type to be built, as D1500, and is now preserved. In the background is Preston Power Box, which was built on the site of the former engine shed.* **Peter Fitton.**

Following the route onwards, the imposing structure of St. Walburge's church towers above the western side of the line. Just under half a mile along is the site of Greenbank Sidings, which were controlled by a signalbox of the same name and lay to the left of the line close to Aqueduct Street. The sidings were sharply curved and it was not possible to use any of the standard LMS or BR shunting locomotives in their environs; instead, a pair of 0-4-0 saddle tanks was kept for these duties. 47002 was built by Kitson & Co in 1932, and classmate 47008 was one of a later but similar batch constructed at Horwich Works. These quirky little locomotives were originally shedded at Preston, later moving to Lostock Hall, but due to their short wheelbase they could often 'disappear' from track circuits and had to be escorted to and from their place of work by another engine! Their use was discontinued in 1966 when the sidings were closed.

The line from Greenbank Sidings northwards was quadrupled in 1903 but the section southwards to Preston remained double track; during the rationalisation in the early 1970s the line was returned to double status apart from two short sections used as goods loops. A little less than half a mile further on was Oxheys Sidings signalbox, which controlled access to the sidings for the cattle market. The 'box dated from 1923, having been built to replace the original 1902 structure that was demolished to make way for the construction of the new Blackpool Road bridge. The cattle market itself dated from 1867 and was finally closed in 2002, but the sidings serving it were lifted in 1968 when livestock traffic was transferred to the roads. A passenger station also existed in this location from 1840 until 1925 when it was closed by the LMS. The signalbox here lingered on until 1973 when its function was ousted by Preston Power Box. A half-mile length of goods loop stretches north from this point.

Continuing north, the popular 60s trainspotting locations of Cadley Causeway, Boys Lane and Lightfoot Lane are passed, the latter being some three miles north of Preston station. Notwithstanding the continual encroachment of housing in the surrounding Fulwood area, open views of the line are still possible in these locations today. Another mile to the north, the site of Barton & Broughton station is passed; this featured on the original Lancaster & Preston Junction Railway and was located just beyond the end of the four-track section from Greenbank Sidings; the northern part of this is marked by the inclusion of a single goods loop. The station was closed to passengers as early as May 1939, but goods facilities remained until May 1965 and even its platforms and waiting shelter survived until then. Though these have since been removed, the station buildings on the down side of the line are still in use today as a private dwelling. Glimpses of the railway's one-time rival, the Lancaster Canal, can be had to the east as trains travel away from Barton.

**Above:** *Ivatt '2MT' 2-6-0 46501 escorts 47002, one of a pair of 0F 0-4-0 saddle tanks kept for shunting the sharply-curved Greenbank Sidings, back to Lostock Hall MPD passing the Durex Felt Works, Dock Street coal yard and site of Preston MPD on 13 February 1963. 47002 was built by Kitson & Co in 1932, and had to be accompanied by another locomotive when on the main line as its diminutive proportions meant that it otherwise frequently 'disappeared' from track circuits!* **Peter Fitton.**

**Below:** *Riddles 'Britannia' class pacific 70020 Mercury drifts the last few hundred yards to the station appraoches from Maudlands on 19 May 1964 with a Class 3 freight in tow. To the left of and above the train can be seen the end of St. Walburge's church, showing just how close the West Coast Main Line passes to this imposing structure.* **Arthur Haymes.**

**Above:** *Stanier Mogul 42970 trundles northwards past Greenbank Sidings with one of the electric units for the Lancaster - Morecambe - Heysham route in tow on 21 March 1961. Just visible in the background to the left is the end of St Walburge's church, with Greenbank Sidings signalbox visible to the rear of the train. The building behind the locomotive is part of Raglan Street Mill.* **Tony Gillett.**

**Below:** *The focusing on this view is slightly soft due to poor weather conditions and the speed of the approaching train, but it is worthy of inclusuion as it illustrates a rare steam-era working of a preserved locomotive on the main line. 7029 Clun Castle, in fictitious GWR livery, thunders northwards past Oxheys sidings on 15 October 1967. The large building visible above the tender of the locomotive is the Empress Cinema on Eldon Street, which closed in the late 1960s.* **Tony Gillett.**

**Above:** *English Electric Type 4 (Class 40) 40 009 heads north at Oxheys in the mid-1970s with a special working containing two ex-LNER wooden-bodied vehicles. The catenary has now appeared and Oxheys sidings have gone; the Empress Cinema still stands, although by this time it had become a roller-skating rink. The houses in the background are on Bucklands Avenue, and the train is about to pass beneath Blackpool Road.* **Peter Fitton.**

**Below:** *Looking in the opposite direction to the previous view, an unidentified Riddles BR Standard Class 5 heads for Preston with a train of milk tankers on 23 May 1964. A classic Ribble bus is just about to cross the line via Blackpool Road bridge, and visible beneath the structure are Oxheys Sidings signalbox and the sidings themselves.* **Arthur Haymes.**

*Stanier 'Princess Coronation' 46239* City of Chester *thunders through Cadley on 21 March 1960 with the down 'Royal Scot'. This train left London Euston at 09:05 and ran non-stop to Carlisle, where a locomotive change took place before the train continued to Glasgow. The safety valves have lifted, so the locomotive has plenty of steam! The bridge over the line here carries Cadley Causeway, while the houses visible in the left distance are on Hillpark Avenue.* **Tony Gillett.**

The line passes beneath the main A6 road, closely paralleled by the canal, through Bilsborrow and shortly afterwards the site of Brock station, around seven miles north of Preston, is passed. Closed to passengers on the same day as Barton & Broughton, it lost its goods traffic in April 1954 and virtually all traces of it have been swept away; just one of the station access path lamps can still be found if you know where to look! A foot crossing traverses the line nearby, close to the site of the new Barton Grange garden centre.

Just north of the station lay Brock water troughs, where most locomotives would lower a scoop to collect water while on the move. In later years, these were not exclusively used by steam traction as many of the then-new diesels would collect water for their train heating boilers. Again, the troughs were a favourite vantage point for watching and photographing trains. An ornate stone arch bridge, complete with stone balusters and adorned with the badger emblem of the Brockholes family of nearby Claughton Hall, crossed the line at this point. However, the beauty and tranquillity of this area has today been forever disfigured following the construction of the M6 motorway that now runs directly to the east of the line here. Its arrival, together with the electrification of the railway, heralded the demolition of the aforementioned stone arch bridge which has now been replaced by a characterless concrete structure, albeit with the badger emblem stones re-used.

After passing through Town Croft Wood on the stretch of line at Claughton-on-Brock, views across the surrounding landscape can be enjoyed; the Lancaster Canal is located immediately next to the line on the western side with the Bowland fells to the east beyond the motorway. Reaching Catterall, the line crosses the River Calder, after which, on the east side of the line, is situated the only 25kV substation for the railway catenary in the Preston area.

Immediately north of this point lies the site of Garstang & Catterall station, which lay high up on an embankment next to Ray Lane; another of the original Lancaster & Preston Junction Railway stations of 1840 it was a late closure under Beeching, succumbing on 3 February 1969. In the 1950s and 60s its goods yard could be a hive of activity; the station was also the junction for the former Garstang & Knott End branch that by that time was closed beyond Pilling.

So far was the site of Garstang & Catterall station from either place its name alluded to that the Garstang & Knott End line followed the route of the main line for over three-quarters of a mile before branching off to the west at Barnacre towards Garstang Town station.

**Above:** *Namesake of the Stanier 'Princess Royal' class Pacifics 46200* The Princess Royal *storms across Sharoe Brook, approaching Lightfoot Lane, with a northbound express on 23 March 1960. As with the 'Duchess' in the previous shot, the locomotive's safety valves are blowing off, suggesting that the fireman has overdone things on the favourable gradients on the stretch immediately north of Preston.* **Tony Gillett**

**Below:** *Stanier 'Black 5' 45446 drifts towards Lightfoot Lane with an up freight on 4 July 1966. The bridge in the background is an occupation bridge for Lightfoot Green Farm. This view has completely changed today, as the M55 motorway crosses the line about where the rear brake van can be seen here.* **Peter Fitton.**

A fireman's eye view of the northbound approach to Barton & Broughton on 7 June 1961 from the footplate of Stanier 'Jubilee' class namesake 45552 Silver Jubilee. The signalbox is on the right, with the bridge carrying Station Lane visible behind. A goods train is held in the loop to the left. **Tony Gillett.**

**Above:** *Stanier 'Jubilee' 45688* Polyphemus *leaves the goods yard at Barton & Brougton and heads onto the up slow line with a mixed freight on 22 March 1961. In addition to controlling access to the goods yard, the signalbox in the background operated the junction where the four tracks from Preston merged into two for the journey north.* **Tony Gillett.**

**Below:** *The view from Station Lane overbridge looking south around 1972. The goods yard has been demolished and four tracks have been reduced to three at this point, though the third is just a goods loop. The signalling has been rationalised accordingly, with the arm having been removed from one of the dolls. The semaphores and signalbox would be swept away soon afterwards.* **Peter Rigby.**

*A view in the other direction around the same time shows the temporary rationalised arrangement here, with the facing crossover controlled from a ground frame. Though the platforms have long gone, the old Lancaster & Preston Junction Railway station building to the left survives in use as a pair of private dwellings to this day.* **Peter Rigby.**

The branch was opened as far as Pilling in 1870, but the final four and a half miles to Knott End were only completed in 1908. With the conclusion of the First World War, a boom in the use of commercial buses brought significant competition for passenger traffic which the branch could not sustain; its last passenger services ran in 1930 and were provided by an outmoded LNWR steam railcar. Goods traffic kept the whole line alive; a salt works at Preesall, between Pilling and Knott End, provided a considerable amount of freight until a pipeline was built to Burn Naze on the other side of the River Wyre estuary. The line beyond Pilling was closed from 13 November 1950, while the section from this point to Garstang Town station followed on 31 July 1963. The remaining one-and-three-quarter mile stretch to Garstang & Catterall finally succumbed on 16 August 1965, after which time the track was lifted. Few traces of the 11 mile line now remain, save for around a mile of footpath on the trackbed near Knott End and a number of bridges on the West Coast Main Line that contain an extra narrow arch on their western side.

Beyond Garstang, the main line reaches the environs of Lancaster, so this is a good time to curtail our examination of the route north and look at other railways in the Preston area.

**Above:** *The tranquillity of the surroundings at Brock water troughs is temporarily disturbed as Rebuilt 'Royal Scot' 46129 The Scottish Horse hurries southwards with an express on 22 June 1960. The setting of this location was forever destroyed with the construction of the Preston to Lancaster section of the M6 in 1965; this now runs through the field behind the train, parallel to the railway.*

**Below:** *A view from the other end of the troughs, taken adjacent to the spotters' favourite location of the so-called 'Badger Bridge' on what is now New Lane. Riddles 9F 92216 has its tender replenished as it takes a morning freight, consisting entirely of containers on 'conflat' wagons, northwards on the West Coast Main Line on 1 September 1965. Note the water tower in the background, which provided the supply necessary to replenish the troughs.* **Both: Peter Fitton.**

**Above:** *The same location as the previous view just nine years later. While the troughs and telegraph poles have gone, this spot is identifiable by the fencing, pylons and Armstrong's Crossing Wood in the background. Brand new Class 87 87 018 heads north at Brock in May 1974 with a special shortened formation of the Royal Train conveying Her Majesty the Queen and the Duke of Edinburgh. Test coach 'Mentor' is immediately behind the locomotive.* **Peter Fitton.**

**Below:** *A stunning portrait of Stanier 'Black 5' 44888 at rest while shunting a pick-up goods at Garstang & Catterall station on 24 July 1968. Despite the fact that there are less than two weeks to go before the end of steam on British Railways, the locomotive appears in good condition and the volunteer cleaners of the MNA - the 'Master Neverers Association' - have clearly been busy!* **Tony Gillett.**

**Above:** *Stanier 'Black 5' 44957 thunders southwards on the approach to Garstang & Catterall station with a fitted freight on 16 July 1966. To the left is the former Knott End branch line, which had remained in use as far as Garstang Town until exactly 11 months previoulsy. There was no physical connection between the Knott End branch and the West Coast Main Line north of the station, although the two routes ran parallel for almost a mile. The building to the right is the Garstang creamery.*

**Below:** *A fine view of Garstang & Catterall station on 28 August 1965, with 'Black 5' 45260 sweeping through at the head of an up express. Obvious pride is being taken with the appearance of the platforms and the parcels operation seems to be thriving, though one wonders at the bravery or foolhardiness of the porter who is casually standing on the rail of the down through line, presumably waiting for the train to pass before he carries his parcel to the up platform!* **Both: Arthur Haymes.**

**Above:** *Jet age technology in a steam age shell! Gas turbine-powered 4-6-0 GT3 stands at the north end of Preston's platform 5 (now 3) on 20 October 1961. The locomotive, which was similar in overall size to a 'Black 5', was built by English Electric at Vulcan Foundry, Newton-le-Willows, between 1958 and 1961 and was under test at the time this photograph was taken. Advances in diesel technology quickly overtook the concept, and GT3 was withdrawn in 1962 and scrapped.* **Tony Gillett.**

**Below:** *An altogether sleeker and more modern appearance is portrayed in the same spot by another English Electric product. DP2 used a Deltic bodyshell but was in fact the prototype Class 50, and the locomotive has paused at Preston with a Euston to Perth express on 28 September 1962. Less than a year separates these two views, illustrating just how dated GT3 had quickly become.* **Peter Fitton.**

**Above:** *A thoroughly unusual prototype test formation is seen at the south end of Preston's platform 4 (originally 6) on 4 July 1978. The set includes one of the former Class 41 prototype HST power cars and one of the APT-P non-driving motor cars, with a brace of departmental Mark 1 coaches completing the rake.*

**Below:** *The one that started it all! Prototype two-car railbus 140 001 stands in platform 5 in June 1981 while undergoing testing. The unit was constructed by British Rail Engineering Limited in Derby almost entirely from Leyland National bus body parts, resulting in a much narrower body than the production series vehicles; only the cab fronts were BR products, and were cut-down versions of those used on the Class 210 DEMUs..* **Both: Dave Felton.**

**Above:** *The unique prototype Class 89, 89 001, approaches Leyland on the Down Fast Line with a test train on 28 September 1987. With 'Test Coach 10' immediately behind the locomotive, the rest of the train consisted of the BREL 'International Stock'. 89001 was built at Crewe in 1986 as a contender for a fleet to be constructed for the then-forthcoming East Coast Main Line electrification. In the event, the Class 91s were chosen for production and the stylish 89 remained a one off.* **Martyn Hilbert.**

**Below:** *Class 91, 91 001, departs Preston with a Carlisle to Crewe test train on 5 June 1988. At this time the East Coast Main Line electrification was still incomplete, and the proving runs were undertaken on the West Coast route. The locomotive was the pioneer of a class that eventually numbered 31 examples, and entered passenger service on 3 March 1989.* **Dave Felton.**

**Above:** *On 17 July 1972, English Electric Type 4 (Class 40) 387 passes Farington Curve Junction signalbox with a northbound permanent way train. Big changes are afoot, as evidenced by the new modern colour light signal with 'feathers' junction indicator, installed immediately beside the old one, behind the locomotive, and the vast array of catenary stanchions.*

**Below:** *It's a similar story in the immediate Preston environs at the same time. A vast new signal gantry has been provided, all its signals installed but blanked off prior to commissioning, and two new lattice supports for the catenary have been erected. Meanwhile, relics of the steam age abound, including No. 1 signalbox and the semaphore signal and gas lamp in the foreground as Brush Type 4 (Class 47) 1863 departs the station with a southbound train.*

**Above:** *By early 1973, the catenary has been installed but is yet to be energised. Work continues on demolition of the old signalling amid the wires as Class 50 419 heads south from Preston with a mere five-coach load. The signalbox seen here at Ribble Siding was a replacement for the life-expired original and lasted a mere 20 years, being abolished on 5 February 1973.*

**Below:** *A close-up view of demolition work underway on the same gantry. A team of Signal & Telegraph engineers strip planking and loose steelwork away, while more stubborn components are merely cut through with an oxy-acetylene torch. Note the rags tied with string to protect the catenary wires from the sharp edges on the gantry. **All: Peter Fitton.***

**Above:** *The scene at Ashton on the Blackpool line, looking towards Preston from alongside Cottam Lane underbridge, following closure of the signalbox in February 1973. The vast space in the foreground was once occupied by the fast lines to Blackpool Central, removed in 1966; the B6241 Tom Benson Way now uses this section of the trackbed.*

**Below:** *The distant arm that once protected the section controlled by Lea Road signalbox plummets to the ground. Soon, the posts and telegraph wires will follow. The S&T engineer seems to be in a very precarious position!* **Both: Peter Fitton.**

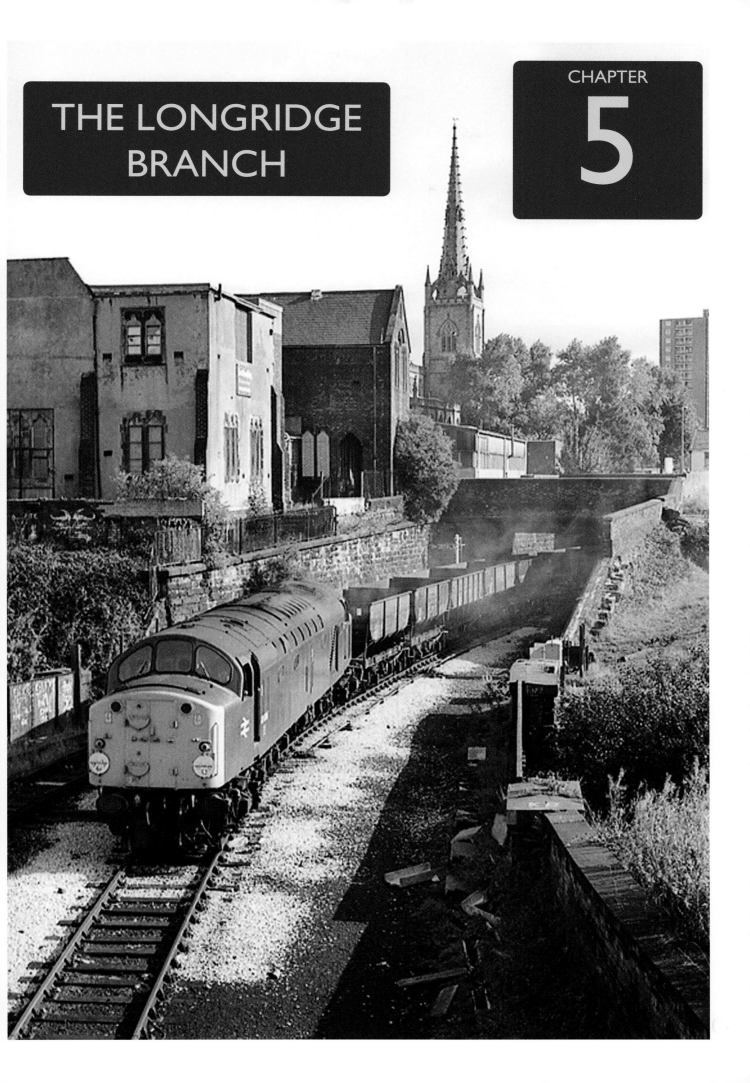

# THE LONGRIDGE BRANCH

**Above:** *Sulzer Type 2 (Class 25) 25 321 has just rounded the severe Maudland Curve linking the Longridge branch with the West Coast Main Line and is crossing over the span that bridged the drained section of the Lancaster Canal. The loco is heading for Deepdale with loaded HEA coal hoppers on 3 May 1985. 25321 was the former D7671 and was the last locomotive built at Derby Works in 1967.* **Martyn Hilbert.**

**Previous page:** *English Electric Type 4s (Class 40s) were a common sight on the surviving stretch of the Longridge branch in the 1970s and early 1980s. Here, 40 096 is heading back towards Preston, having collected a load of hoppers from Deepdale Street on 12 September 1983. The train has just passed under Cold Bath Street and is about to cross the disused section of the Lancaster Canal.* **Tony Woof.**

Plans for a plateway or railway to serve the bustling stone quarries in the Longridge area started in the early 1830s, shortly after the principal routes around Preston began to appear. At the time the durable millstone grit known as Ashlar (but more commonly called Longridge stone) was in great demand for building projects, but the quantities of the material that could be produced by the newly-opened quarries were severely limited by the primitive horse and cart transportation then available.

In the mid-1830s, the expansion of the Liverpool dock system began, calling for vast amounts of Ashlar to be transported from the Longridge quarries. Clearly, using horses to haul large blocks of stone weighing anything up to five tons on the dirt roads that existed at the time was an unsatisfactory and time-consuming exercise. With the prospect of a vast increase in production on the horizon, the Preston & Longridge Railway Company was formed with the aim of building a line to transport materials between the two towns, a distance of around six and a half miles. At this time, the rest of the railway network in the Preston area (with the exception of the Lancaster Canal tramroad) had yet to be built, and the route surveyed was to leave the Preston terminus remote from the other lines for several years.

Construction began in 1835 but progress was extremely slow and the line between Tootal Heights quarries and the Deepdale area of Preston was not completed until 1840; the official opening taking place on 1 May. The route was via Grimsargh, Gammull Lane and Ribbleton, with the terminus in Deepdale Street (not to be confused with Deepdale Road, where a later station was provided) on the opposite side to where the Halfords store stands today. The trains were pulled by horses at the outset, the intention being to introduce locomotives if the traffic demand made the expense worthwhile. Unsurprisingly, the line was almost totally given over to freight with just two passenger trains each way per week, one on Thursdays and another on Saturdays. Special trains could be organised if enough spare horses were available, although in many cases passengers simply rode in the trucks with the stone! Things improved somewhat with the passing of the 1844 Railway Regulation Act, with the company (in common with all other railways) obliged to provide a minimum of one passenger working per day in each direction, complete with covered accommodation for all classes - no longer was conveyance by stone truck deemed adequate!

**Above:** *Seen from a vantage point beneath Cold Bath Street bridge in 1974, a coal train from Courtaulds makes its way beneath the bridges at the western end of the 'Miley Tunnel' in the charge of English Electric Type 4 40 166. Pollard Street (nearest the camera) and Radnor Street bridges are identifiable here, with the Fylde Road tunnel portal beyond.* **Tom Sutch.**

**Below:** *One of the gaps in the 'Miley Tunnel' is evident in this November 1964 view from the 'six foot' by the western portal of the section running beneath Moor Lane. The open section of cutting visible runs between Adelphi Place (on the left) and St. Peter's Street, while the short tunnel beyond the cutting walls runs beneath Adelphi Street and Fylde Road.* **Tony Gillett.**

*This November 1976 view depicts the bridge carrying Deepdale Road over the Longridge Branch. By this time the line had been singled and Deepdale station, visible through the arch, was in the process of being demolished. Just faintly discernable in the distance is the footbridge linking Porter Street with Castleton Road; St. Paul's Road bridge is a short distance behind the photographer, and, a few hundred yards beyond that, the eastern portal of the 'Miley Tunnel'.* **Dave Felton.**

From these inauspicious beginnings came grand plans; perhaps the most ambitious of these being that of the grandly-titled Fleetwood, Preston & West Riding Junction Railway (FP&WRJR), which planned to link the Preston & Wyre line from the Fylde to the Yorkshire coalfields and the market town of Skipton by way of the Preston & Longridge line. Work began on the new route in 1847 when excavation of the lengthy cutting at Deepdale commenced near the site of the former infirmary (today given over to housing and a small retail park). The cutting was originally intended to stretch between the Preston & Lancaster line at Maudlands to Skeffington Road, a distance of around 1200 yards, but due to the quantity of spoil generated and the problems experienced in disposing of it, the decision was made to provide three tunnels at the western end (today known to locals as one structure - the 'Miley Tunnel') with a total length of 862 yards. The cutting was excavated to double-track width, and at the same time the section of existing line between Deepdale and Grimsargh was doubled. Works to extend the route towards Clitheroe also began in 1847 with the excavation of a shallow 250-yard cutting at Hurst Green. However, further funds were not forthcoming and the extension at the Longridge end was subsequently abandoned.

As part of the FP&WRJR scheme, provision was made to permit locomotive working on the branch, and the first steam-hauled trains ran in 1848. The route through the new cutting to Maudlands was finally opened in 1850, by which time all hope of extending the line into Yorkshire had vanished. At this time the Longridge branch was linked directly to the Preston & Wyre line, crossing the main line to Lancaster on the level. This less than satisfactory arrangement resulted in some near misses and the occasional dramatic accident!

With the failure of the FP&WRJR scheme, the company quickly became bankrupt but was resurrected in 1856 and formally purchased the Longridge branch. Under ownership of the new company significant improvements were made; a new station was opened at Maudland Bridge, with another at Deepdale Bridge (adjacent to the stone-built bridge in Deepdale Road) provided shortly afterwards. With the opening of the latter station, the former terminus in Deepdale Street was closed to passengers and devoted solely to goods traffic. By 1860, the company was in good financial health and five passenger trains were operated each way per day using good quality (and in some cases brand new) locomotives and rolling stock.

**Above:** *The once-grand station buiding at Deepdale Bridge in the course of demolition in November 1976. The bricked-up doorway on the first storey led to a footbridge across to the Longridge-bound platform. Much of the building was used as the offices and headquarters of the FP&WRJR following closure of Deepdale Street to passengers. The rear edge of the attractive Deepdale Road facade can be seen jutting out onto the bridge; following closure to passengers this served as a fruiterers stores for many years.* **Dave Felton.**

**Below:** *Making a change from the staple coal traffic that was seen on the branch at the time, Class 25 25 297 heads a mixed rake of wagons through the site of the long closed Deepdale Station in June 1978. The train had originated at Maudland Goods Yard and was heading for Deepdale Junction to allow the locomotive to run round.* **Martyn Hilbert.**

**Above:** *With the rear of the houses on Castleton Road as a backdrop, a pair of work-stained Class 20s, 20 042 and 20 209, plod slowly along the former Longridge Branch towards Porter Street Footbridge with a lengthy coal train on 16 May 1986. Trains to the coal depot at Deepdale normally worked in the morning, though on this occasion it ran in the afternoon.*

**Below:** *Embellished with a silver roof, Brush Type 4 (Class 47) 47 277 grinds its way through Deepdale with a train of loaded HEA wagons from Toton Yard on 22 June 1987. In the background is the former Preston Royal Infirmary which closed its doors for the last time in 1981; all the mill chimneys visible here have also gone.* **Both: Martyn Hilbert.**

*Sulzer Type 2 (Class 25) 25 181 approaches Deepdale Junction with a train of loaded HEA coal hoppers bound for Deepdale Street coal concentration yard on 12 April 1985, having worked the train from Arpley Yard in Warrington. Hawkhurst Road bridge is visible in the background.* **Martyn Hilbert.**

In 1866, plans were again mooted to extend the line into Yorkshire, but this failed to come to fruition, much to the relief of the Lancashire & Yorkshire Railway; the latter company promptly taking over the line jointly with the London & North Western Railway, with the FP&WRJR becoming defunct from 1867. At the time of the takeover, the L&YR were responsible for providing the trains while the LNWR were in charge of the permanent way. Passenger stations then consisted of Maudland Bridge, Deepdale Bridge, Fulwood (previously Gammer Lane, opened in 1854) and Longridge, the latter on a different site to the building that survives at the present time. A stopping place (though not a 'proper' station) was also in use at Grimsargh adjacent to the Plough Hotel; this was formalised in 1870 when the joint companies provided a new station. In the same year, facilities at Longridge were improved with the provision of a new station that was partially built onto the side of the Towneley Arms Hotel, and this survives to this day. The dangerous situation arising from the crossing of the main line on the level at the Preston end of the branch was remedied in 1885 with the provision of Maudland Curve, which diverted all trains into the new joint station at Preston. Maudland Bridge station was closed and demolished in the same year.

Under the auspices of the joint companies the branch was initially quite busy and was progressively improved and modernised over the years. Semaphore signalling (to the LNWR standard) was introduced from 1882, with new signalboxes provided at Longridge and Deepdale Junction (where the goods line to the former Deepdale Street station diverged). A further signalbox was added at Maudlands with the opening of the new curve in 1885. The prosperity lasted until the outbreak of the First World War, after which time traffic began to decline significantly. By the end of the war, the quarrying industry in the area was in dire straits thanks to the mass production of bricks, which were now used in the vast majority of building projects. Surprisingly, the passenger traffic that had initially been frowned upon by the Preston & Longridge Company was thriving, and was more than sufficient to ensure the line's survival. Such was the state of affairs when the route was absorbed by the LMS at the Grouping in 1923, though under their ownership the line's fortunes declined and services were run down. Eventually the LMS decided to withdraw passenger trains on the branch, which ceased with effect from 2 June 1930.

For the next few years goods trains continued to serve the stations, factories and goods yards along the line. In 1938, Messrs. Courtaulds Limited opened a rayon factory, to which the railway supplied large quantities of coal on a daily basis. A decade later when British Railways took over the line, two goods trains traversed the branch on weekdays; this was reduced to one train per day in the 1950s.

**Above:** *The train crew have gone to open the level crossing gates at Skeffington Road, as Cardiff Canton allocated English Electric Type 3 (Class 37) 37 222 stands at Deepdale Junction with a rake of loaded HEA coal hoppers in July 1991. The train will run forwards over the level crossing, then reverse back along what was the original Preston & Longridge route seen on the right of this view to access the coal depot built on the site of the original passenger terminus.* **Martyn Hilbert.**

**Below:** *Sulzer Type 2 (Class 25) 25 248 waits at Deepdale Junction with a rake of coal wagons that it is bringing down the short line from Deepdale Street coal yard on 27 August 1982.* **Tony Woof.**

**Above:** *Heading up the branch from Deepdale Junction to the coal sidings, a further level crossing is reached at Deepdale Mill Street. Having worked from Toton Yard via Warrington, a pair of class 20s, 20 056 and 20 072 wait for the gates to be opened before propelling the two loaded HEA coal hoppers to the coal yard on 24 May 1985.* **Martyn Hilbert.**

**Below:** *Deepdale Mill Street crossing was provided with accommodation for the crossing keeper from the opening of the Preston & Longridge line in 1840. This was the scene on 4 November 1988, with the derelict crossing keeper's house up to let. Inevitably, all three buildings on this row have now been demolished.* **Dave Felton.**

**Above:** *Class 40 40 002 slowly reverses its train of empty 21 ton coal hoppers across Deepdale Mill Street Level Crossing on 15 August 1983. Once the train has reached Deepdale Junction, the locomotive will haul the empties to Healey Mills Yard near Wakefield.* **Martyn Hilbert.**

**Below:** *The view down to Deepdale Junction from the Deepdale Street spur in steam days, taken from the cab of Stanier '8F' 48002 in September 1965. The train is just crossing Deepdale Mill Street, beyond which can be glimpsed Deepdale Junction signalbox. Skeffington Road crossing lies a few hundred yards east of the junction. Note the LNWR lower quadrant semaphore signals.* **Tony Gillett.**

*Class 37 37 222, based at Cardiff Canton Depot, is a long way from home as it stands among the weeds at Deepdale on 25 July 1991. The locomotive was about to push its train of empty HEA coal hoppers back towards Deepdale Junction ready for the onward journey to Washwood Heath Yard in Birmingham.* **Martyn Hilbert.**

As the only line in the Preston area without a train service on Sundays, the Longridge line was ideally suited as a test route for new locomotives for the nearby English Electric works on Strand Road in Preston and famous engines such as DP1, the prototype 'Deltic', had a number of outings on the branch.

With the dawn of the 1960s things were in decline for the railways in general. A sign of things to come was the dissection of the line by the M6 Preston Bypass, the first motorway to be built in Britain; a new bridge was built to carry the line over the four (later six) lanes of ugly asphalt. With the publication of the infamous Beeching Report it is perhaps surprising that the Longridge branch survived as long as it did. Goods traffic was formally withdrawn beyond the Courtaulds siding on 6 November 1967, though the last actual working from the terminus took place on 5 March 1968 when a locomotive was sent to collect a solitary wagon that had been used to transport a load of cinders to repair a railway path. Courtaulds continued to receive one coal train per day, with the former Deepdale Street terminus also surviving in use as a coal concentration yard.

The Courtaulds factory itself closed in 1980 and the remaining section of line between its sidings and Deepdale was lifted. The remainder survived to provide access to the coal yard in Deepdale Street, with a shunting neck extending to a point behind the present West View Leisure Centre in Ribbleton. The last coal trains ran on the branch in 1994 but thankfully the track remains in situ at the time of writing, albeit in a heavily-overgrown 'mothballed' state. The bridge over the motorway was demolished when the M6 was widened to eight lanes in the early 1990s, and replaced by a footbridge to carry the path that now follows much of the route. There are currently plans to install catenary along the surviving section of the line and use it as a test bed for a light rail system; it is hoped the latter may eventually run throughout the Preston area. In the author's opinion, reinstatement of a conventional rail service is much more suitable!

### The Whittingham Hospital Railway

The 'no fare train' is often lamented by Preston residents who can remember a unique little railway that existed for a little under seven decades. Construction of the County Mental Asylum at Whittingham, near Goosnargh, began in 1869 and, following subsequent enlargement a decade later, had capacity to accommodate around 2,900 patients. Much like the Longridge quarries some 40 years before, they were struggling to have supplies delivered on the inadequate roads of the day and proposed a railway to link the hospital site with the Longridge branch at Grimsargh.

**Above:** *Leaving Deepdale Junction behind we continue our journey towards Longridge. Today, the track ends behind West View Leidure Centre in Ribbleton, but in happier times (4 July 1966 in fact) we see Stanier '8F' 48438 passing beneath the ornate bridge carrying Cromwell Road across the line. The locomotive is returning towards Preston with empty 16-ton coal wagons from Courtaulds rayon works.* **Peter Fitton.**

**Below:** *With no weekend working in the late 1960s, the end of steam on the former Longridge branch came on Friday 2 August 1968. Stanier 'Black 5', adorned with suitably poignant messages on the smokebox door, undertakes the last ever steam duty as it collects a rake of coal empties from Courtaulds.* **David Eaves.**

**Above:** *English Electric Type 4 40 166 rolls onto a rake of empty 16-ton mineral wagons in the exchange sidings at Courtaulds, having just delivered a train loaded with coal for the rayon works.* **Tom Sutch.**

**Below:** *Sulzer Type 2 25 142 slowly draws the last train of empty 16-ton mineral wagons on to the remains of the former Preston to Longridge line on 12 February 1980. This was the last train ever to work along the section of line from Ribbleton to Deepdale. The locomotive has a backdrop of open fields - this area is now redeveloped with an M6 Motorway link road and an industrial estate.* **Martyn Hilbert.**

**Above:** *A scene in Courtaulds exchange sidings in September 1965 with one of the works' Peckett steam locomotives (Works. No. 2086) waiting to collect a rake of coal wagons. An '8F' is about to depart with a train of empties that the Peckett has delivered from the factory.* **Tony Gillett.**

**Below:** *The resident Courtaulds diesel shunter, Sentinel 10280 built in 1968 is seen passing under the bridge carrying the B6243 Preston to Longridge main road on 12 February 1980. The works was connected to the truncated remains of the Longridge Branch by a one mile connecting spur. This was the last day of work at Preston for this locomotive; following closure of the factory it moved to the British Celanese Plant at Spondon.* **Martyn Hilbert.**

**Above:** *Though closed to passengers in 1930, the occasional special ventured down the branch in the 1950s and 60s. Springs Branch (Wigan) based LNWR 'Super D' 49451 approaches Grimsargh en route to Longridge with the RCTS 'Mid-Lancs Railtour' on 22 September 1962.* **Peter Fitton.**

**Below:** *The view looking towards Longridge from the station platform at Grimsargh in November 1964. Though it had been closed to passengers for well over three decades its appearance was still tidy, though the crossing gates have seen better days! The Whittingham Hospital Railway station, closed in 1957, can be seen to the left across the road. All traces of both stations have now been completely obliterated.* **Tony Gillett.**

*Longridge railway station was built onto the side of the Towneley Arms and was located on the Preston side of Berry Lane level crossing. The goods yard, together with the defunct line to the quarries, was located on the opposite side of the road and we see the station from the cab of an unidentified Class 08 shunter which is about to work a trip freight towards Preston.* **Tony Gillett.**

Construction of the 2,863 yard line began in 1887 but a number of problems were experienced, including inclement weather causing slipping of the embankments; the line therefore did not begin operating until 1889, initially for goods only. A station was provided at Grimsargh, separated from the Longridge branch one by the level crossing and on the opposite side of the line. A trailing connection was provided between the two branches to enable wagons to be transferred in either direction. At the Whittingham end of the line, an ornate station was provided complete with overall iron and glass roof, and was certainly better appointed than many small stations on the main line! From here, the line continued to a siding and the hospital boiler house.

From the outset, the Whittingham line provided its own locomotives, the first being an Andrew Barclay & Sons 0-4-0 saddle tank of standard design, many examples of which can be seen on the Preston-based Ribble Steam Railway today. This locomotive was built in 1888, and was joined at Whittingham by an 0-4-2 side tank from the same manufacturer in 1904; these lasted until 1947 and 1952 respectively, both being scrapped. As a replacement, the hospital purchased secondhand an ex-London Brighton & South Coast Railway Stroudley D1 class 0-4-2T, which arrived in 1947 and was named *James Friars* after the Hospital Management Committee chairman. This was older than both the locomotives it replaced, dating from 1886, and unsurprisingly was withdrawn with serious boiler defects in 1956. A further secondhand locomotive, this time a 100hp Sentinel 0-4-0 vertical boilered tank, was acquired from Bolton gasworks and named *Gradwell*. Though small, this plucky little engine proved reliable and more than adequate for the line's needs.

The decision to carry passengers was made early on in the line's history, following a number of petitions from both visitors and staff. A handful of four-wheeled coaches were used for much of the line's life, though in later years these were replaced by a rake of three vehicles converted from former LNWR goods brake vans. A fare was never charged throughout the railway's existence, and travel was available for anyone wishing to make the journey - not just those travelling to the hospital. The line carried more than 3,000 passengers per week at the height of operations just after the First World War, and at the same time carried more than 12,000 tons of freight per year. The passenger service survived the withdrawal of the one on the Longridge branch and trains were re-timed to connect with the bus services at Grimsargh. Nonetheless, with declining economic fortunes the decision was made to close the line with effect from 30 June 1957, after which the track was quickly lifted. Whittingham Hospital has itself now closed and housing has been built both on this site and on that of Grimsargh station. With more houses still to be built at Whittingham and the surrounding roads in Broughton, Longridge and Fulwood stretched to breaking point, one can't help but wonder if obliterating the trackbed is a sensible idea, or whether reinstating some form of rail transport to these locations may be the cure for the serious congestion experienced today.

**Above:** *The level crossing is closed to cars in this view of the station on 25 September 1965, with Stanier 8F 48002 taking water from the tower. The provision of a platform trolley suggests that parcels traffic was still in evidence at this time. The compact signalbox is visible to the left.* **Tony Gillett.**

**Below:** *LNWR G2a 'Super D' 49451 has run round its train at Longridge station and is preparing to return towards Preston with the RCTS 'Mid Lancs Railtour' on 25 September 1962. The arrival of a passenger working has clearly aroused the interest of several of the town's younger residents!* **Peter Fitton.**

**Above:** *The end of the line for the Whittingham Hospital Railway came on 29 June 1957; Sentinel 0-4-0VBT* Gradwell *is seen heading the last working, the 19:20 departure from Grimsargh, towards the hospital.* **Peter Fitton.**

**Below:** *The Whittingham terminus of the hospital line was quite ornate, complete with an iron and glass overall roof, and was built on a curve. In this view taken in September 1969, the track has gone but the building is still largely intact. Remnants can still be seen today, though the whole site is now thickly covered with trees.* **Tony Gillett.**

# THE RIBBLE BRANCH TO PRESTON DOCK

**Above:** *Steam ended on the Britsih Railways section of the Ribble Branch in 1959, after which time the English Electric Type 4, later known as the Class 40, was the staple motive power. On 23 October 1975, 40 171 descends the bank towards Strand Road with a coal train from Parkside Colliery. The locomotive is framed by the portal of Christian Road bridge; as indicated by the level board on the left of the picture, this is the point where the 1-in-29 gradient from the station changes to a slightly more gentle 1-in-55!* **Tom Sutch.**

**Previous page:** *The route taken by the Ribble Branch between Preston station approaches and Strand Road is a difficult one for the unfamiliar eye to trace. It drops steeply immediately after branching off the main line, passing beneath Christian Road in an extremely narrow brick-and-stone-lined cutting. Until 1972, its descent was further hidden by Preston No. 2A signalbox, which straddled the track and was located in the gap in the wall visible to the right of the line.* **Tom Sutch.**

## Origins of the system

The Ribble Navigation Company was formed in 1806 to improve the River Ribble, which until that time took a fairly meandering course between the sea and the town of Preston. Over the next thirty years or so, a series of training walls were constructed to straighten it until it followed the course it does today as far as the dock entrance. The improvements were successful in opening up the river to shipping.

The Ribble Navigation Company entered its second incarnation in 1838, and Preston legally became a properly functioning port with the construction of the Victoria Quay, located at the bottom of Marsh Lane, in 1843. Traffic increased, and in 1846 a railway was constructed to improve the prosperity of the new facilities.

The new line, constructed by the North Union Railway and jointly controlled by that company and the Ribble Navigation Company, left what is now the West Coast Main Line to the south of Preston station. Descending sharply at 1 in 29 to drop beneath Christian Road and West Cliff in a narrow brick-lined cutting, it then passed beneath Fishergate Hill in a tunnel, from which it emerged shortly before Hartington Road. A level crossing took the line across Strand Road, after which it became the sole property of the Navigation Company.

**Above:** *Another coal train for the power station is seen passing beneath Waltons Parade on 21 October 1975. The large open area to the right of the train is now heavily overgrown. The portal of Fishergate Hill tunnel is directly behind the photographer.*

**Below:** *The same train is seen on the short stretch of line between the southern tunnel portal at Hartington Road (the end of which can just be glimpsed above the rearmost visible wagon) and Strand Road crossing. The locomotive in charge on this day is 40 177. Note the redundant piers that once carried a bridge over the line at this point. **Both: Tom Sutch.***

**Above:** *An unidentified Class 47 rumbles slowly over Strand Road crossing to enter the dock railway system. Note the man with the red flag - the only traffic management deemed necessary for stopping road vehicles on this busy 4-lane road, even in the mid-1980s!*

**Below:** *56 065 leaves the dock system exchange sidings with a train of petrol tankers. This photograph dates from around 1984 and shows the original alignment of the line before it was re-routed away from Strand Road. Note the corrugated iron fence in the background, which bore the legend 'PORT OF PRESTON'.* **Both: Martyn Hilbert.**

## The branch and dock develop

With ship sizes ever-increasing, improvements to the river channel continued through the second half of the 19th century. The idea of a dock proper was first proposed in 1861, and twenty years of negotiations finally bore fruit in 1883 with the passing of the Ribble Navigation and Preston Dock Act, which effectively transferred the operation into the ownership of Preston Corporation and authorised the construction of a large wet dock. The dock basin was to be built on the course of the River Ribble itself, and this necessitated the diversion of the river to the south.

Work on the construction of the dock began in 1884 with the river diversion works, the 'Diversion Quay' being opened at the east end of the new route as part of the first phase as the Victoria Quay was swallowed up by the construction of the basin. The foundation stone was laid in 1885 and the new dock was formally opened on 25th June 1892 by Prince Albert, Duke of Edinburgh; at that time it was the largest single dock in the country.

The railway was re-laid to serve the Diversion Quay during construction, passing between the site of the new dock and the diverted River Ribble. Once the dock was open to traffic, a line was added to the north side of the basin; this would eventually become the main hub of the dock system.

Trade using the dock grew slowly, with only four ships being unloaded in the opening year; however, within eight years that number had increased to 170. The traffic handled initially by the Port of Preston included timber, china clay, bananas, cattle and cotton, and in 1914 oil storage tanks were constructed on the north side of the dock. Later that year with the onset of the Great War, the dock busied itself with the export of munitions – almost all of which were transported to the port by rail. The years 1914 – 1918 correspondingly marked a high point for traffic that was not equalled for over three decades.

Between the wars, the dock struggled due to the difficult financial times, failing to make a profit. Nonetheless, the rail connection was continually busy. A power station was established across the river at Penwortham in the mid 1920s, with coal for the furnaces brought down the dock branch and sent from the sidings by Diversion Quay across the river using a series of buckets suspended from a cable. The power station was enlarged in 1947, at which time the cross-river transportation was improved by the construction of a conveyor.

**Below:** *In the 1980s the dock estate began to be redeveloped. Just a few yards along the line from the previous shot, Borough of Preston-owned Sentinel* Progress *stands at the exchange sidings awaiting the arrival of tankers from Lindsey refinery. To the left can be seen the new river bridge and the future route for the railway under construction.* **Martyn Hilbert.**

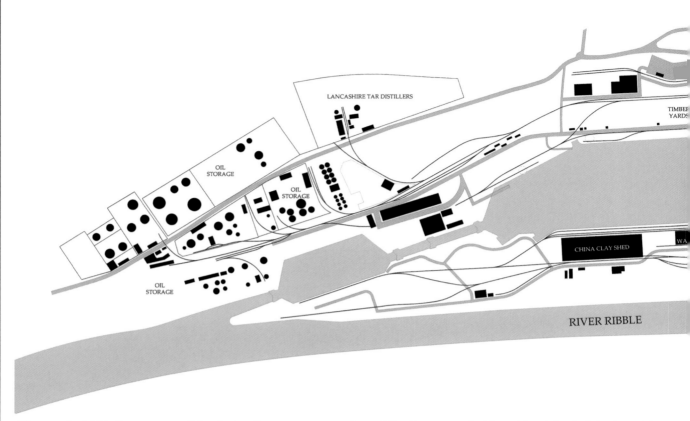

**Above:** *In 1960, the expanse of the dock railway system was huge! The lines spread either side of the dock basin, with some 28 miles of track in total. The oil storage area was considerable, with most of the major companies - including BP, Mobil, Esso Petrofina and Regent all having their own individual compounds. The timber yards took up almost half the length of one side of the basin, and there was also a large timber storage shed adjacent to the exchange sidings.* **Author.**

**Below:** *Bagnall 0-6-0ST* Princess *shunts a short rake of wagons at the end of the northern exchange sidings outside the Victoria Warehouses. This building was located at the bottom of Marsh Lane, but was demolished when the Penwortham Bypass extension was added in the 1980s. The stone name board that can be seen atop the building is now displayed outside a dockside car dealership.* **Trevor Machell.**

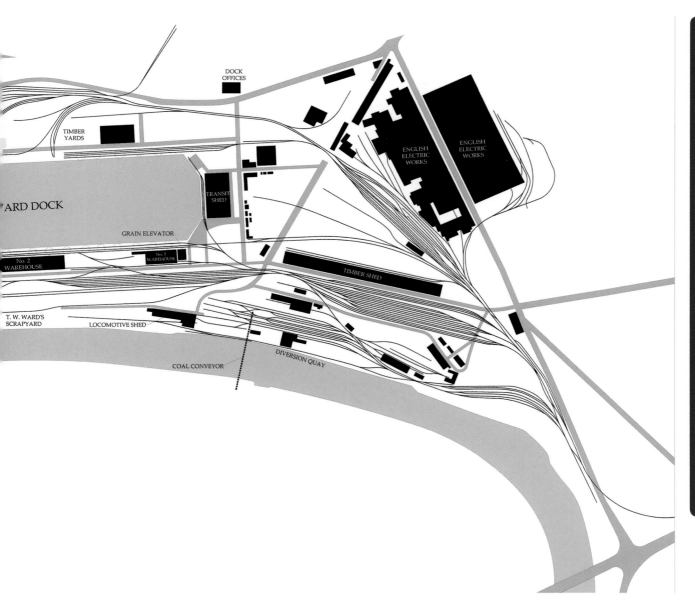

The busy dock railway was worked by an assortment of locomotives, including 1893-built Hawthorn Leslie 0-6-0 saddle tank *Edinburgh* and a Peckett 0-6-0 *Queen* dating from 1906. A fireless locomotive, Andrew Barclay 0-6-0 *Duke*, was purchased in 1937 for working the petrol trains around the rapidly expanding oil storage facility operated by Russian Oil Products (later Regent and then Petrofina). An Armstrong-Whitworth diesel shunter was bought second-hand by Preston Corporation in 1935 and named Duchess. Its success was mixed, as it regularly derailed on the system's tight curves and complex pointwork and its transmission also gave trouble; consequently it spent as much time out of traffic as it did at work!

Following the Second World War, business on the dock was booming and a fleet of more modern locomotives was deemed necessary to work the expansive dock railway system, which at its height consisted of some 28 miles of track. While the diesel shunter *Duchess* survived into the 1960s, its problematic operation ensured that no more orders for similar traction would be made until much later. Instead, further 0-6-0 saddle tanks were ordered from Bagnall, being delivered in the 1940s. Included were *Progress*, *Princess*, *Enterprise*, *Energy*, *Courageous*, *Conqueror* and *Perseverance*. These plucky and powerful locomotives, alongside *Duke* and *Duchess*, worked all the trains on the dock estate from the exchange sidings westwards for more than two further decades.

Modernisation might have been the order of the day on the post-war Preston Corporation-owned section, but on the branch from the exchange sidings to the main line and beyond the LMS and British Railways placed the freight in the charge of venerable London & North Western Railway 'Super D' 0-8-0s. Three of these locomotives were shedded at Preston specifically for these duties, and a pair would normally be required to lift the heavy freight trains up the steep incline towards the station. Coal trains heading to the dock were often in the charge of a single 'Super D', or possibly an even older Aspinall 'A' class 0-6-0; working an unfitted coal train down the steep line must have required great skill and nerves of steel!

**Above:** *Seen at rest near the timber shed on 15 March 1961 are Preston Corporation Bagnall saddle tanks* Courageous *and* Perseverance. *Note the spark arresters fitted on the chimney of each locomotive - while they were never used to shunt the petrol tankers, they each spent a great deal of time in and around the timber yards.* **Tony Gillett.**

**Below:** *Rounding the sharp curve from the transit shed with a mixed freight in summer 1967 is Bagnall 0-6-0ST* Enterprise. *The train is just passing over the level crossing in front of the grain elevator; the end of the dock basin is visible to the left of the picture.* **Trevor Machell.**

**Above:** *An unidentified Bagnall is coupled to a lengthy freight on the south-east corner of the dock. Many of the wagons towards the rear appear to contain china clay; while this type of traffic is normally associated with Cornwall, large quantities were landed at Preston, and were stored and dried in a large shed at the south-west corner of the dock basin. This scene gives a good impression of the exceedingly busy nature of the dock in the late 1960s, with a variety of shipping visible. The grain elevator can be seen to the left.* **Trevor Machell.**

## Boom years

Tar traffic began to appear on the branch in the 1950s with the opening of Lancashire Tar Distillers' site on Chain Caul Road to the north of the dock. The shape of things to come, in the form of road traffic, began to be sent to Ireland from the dock from 1948 when the first 'Roll on, Roll off' ferries were pioneered from the port. Initially, redundant World War II landing craft were used but business improved so much that a purpose-built vehicle ferry was introduced from 1957.

Steam ended on the British Railways section of the branch in 1959, after which time Class 40s were the favourite choice of motive power owing to their great weight giving improved braking for downhill trains and better grip for uphill ones. However, a wide variety of diesel traction soon began to appear, including Class 20s, 25s and even Class 08 shunters. One notable point to mention is that the prototype English Electric Deltic was the first main line diesel locomotive to work along the branch; it was constructed at its manufacturer's works on Strand Road and made its way to the main network via the dock system.

As steam eked out its final existence on the national network, a similar occurrence was taking place on the dock line and in 1968 the final steam workings were made. Thankfully, in that year traffic using the dock was at its busiest level ever, and despite the rapid growth in road traffic the rail connection was seen as vital. The entire fleet of steam locomotives was replaced by just three Rolls Royce-powered Sentinel 4-wheel diesel shunters. These were given the nameplates from *Progress*, *Energy* and *Enterprise* and, unlike *Duchess*, were very successful. Initially painted green like the steam locomotives they replaced, they were soon daubed all over in yellow to improve their conspicuousness. Of the dock's fleet of locomotives, only *Princess* survived into preservation; this locomotive is now based on the Lakeside and Haverthwaite Railway in Cumbria.

**Above:** *The Armstrong Whitworth diesel shunter* Duchess *shunts a rake of Preston Corporation opens in the extensive sidings between the warehouses and the Diversion Quay on a sunny summer day in the mid-1960s. The sheer bulk of the grain elevator is apparent in this shot.* **Trevor Machell.**

## Decline

The dock's Indian Summer was short-lived, the Dockers' Strikes of 1969 and 1970 hitting business hard, with foreign freight affected in particular. Ships continued to increase in size, meaning that not only could fewer use the dock, but also that more dredging of the river was needed to prevent silting up of the channel. With the tidal approach adding further complications for shipping, by 1975 the dock was in decline. In 1979, things had reached breaking point and a proposal was made to close the port; this was formally completed on 31st October 1981. Fortunately, Petrofina and Lancashire Tar Distillers still required rail access, ensuring the survival of the line, and coal trains also continued to supply Penwortham power station until it closed in 1983.

With the closure of the dock, the whole expansive area of 383 acres was designated a redevelopment site. In 1985 a plan was agreed upon and work commenced. To the north of the dock, new roads were to be constructed together with a large retail development. By this time, the only functioning section of the railway was that serving Lancashire Tar Distillers and Petrofina, and this ran rather inconveniently through the middle of the proposed development area. At the time, the amount of traffic attracted by these two industries was considered too great to switch to road transport, so there was no prospect of removing the rail link altogether.

Instead, the railway was relaid on a completely new formation to the south of the dock basin, following the river bank for most of its length from Strand Road crossing and thereby skirting the edge of any future developments on the south side of the basin. With proposals afoot to redevelop the dock itself to cater for leisure craft, a combined road and rail swing bridge was constructed to allow trains to cross the dock entrance and access the truncated stub of the old system. With the new roads planned, a total of three additional road crossings were installed, protected at either end by catch points with the whole arrangement controlled from a new control tower constructed at the south west of the dock basin. A fan of three exchange sidings was constructed at the eastern end of the new railway formation, of sufficient length to allow eighteen bogie tanks to be accommodated. A new engine shed was built at the western end of the line to house the three Sentinel shunters. The old line to the north of the dock was lifted in 1985.

**Above:** *A rare shot of the fireless locomotive* Duke *and Bagnall 0-6-0ST* Conqueror, *both by now withdrawn and devoid of nameplates, standing outside the dockside engine shed on a wet 9 March 1968.* **Tony Gillett.**

**Below:** *In addition to the seven Bagnalls, plus the fireless* Duke *and the temperamental* Duchess, *one other locomotive could be found on the docks in the 1960s. This was a Robert Stephenson & Hawthorns 0-4-0ST, and was used as the yard shunter in T. W. Ward's scrapyard adjacent to the Diversion Quay. This locomotive, too, had a chimney top spark arrester fitted, though there is no evidence it ever worked beyond the confines of the scrapyard itself. Visible in the background across the river is Penwortham Power Station.* **Trevor Machell.**

*Preston Corporation took delivery of the three Rolls Royce-engined Sentinel 4-wheel diesel shunters in 1968. Despite their diminutive size they proved surprisingly powerful. Visible in this shot are* Progress *and* Energy. Progress *survives on the last vestiges of the dock system to this day, while* Energy *was sold but has now been replaced with an identical locomotive that was originally based on the Manchester Ship Canal system.* **Trevor Machell.**

## Rescue

The new line handled up to nine trains each way per week, delivering petrol to Petrofina and bitumen to Lancashire Tar Distillers. However, Petrofina closed its Preston storage depot in 1992, with the tanks being demolished soon afterwards. Thereafter, three trains each way per week continued to be worked along the branch to the bitumen plant. During roadworks on Hartington Road in 1995, the bridge over the railway line was damaged from above by over-zealous digging, closing the branch for several months and leaving the tar distillery reliant on road transport. When the bridge was finally repaired, reorganisation at Lancashire Tar Distillers led to the decision not to return the inbound freight to rail transport, spelling an end to almost a century and a half of continuous operation.

Fortunately, the preservation society once based at Steamport, the erstwhile engine shed near Chapel Street station in Southport, relocated to the line, forming the Ribble Steam Railway. A museum and workshop were constructed on the site of part of the former Petrofina fuel storage depot, and the line opened to the public for steam-hauled passenger trains for the first time in 2005.

Adding to this success story, a joint effort by the Ribble Steam Railway and Lanfina / Total, who now operate the Lancashire Tar Distillers site on Leeward road, saw a government grant awarded and revenue-earning freight back on the branch with the return of the thrice-weekly bitumen trains in 2008. This entailed the upgrade of the level crossing at Strand Road; trains had previously crossed this busy 4-lane highway with the only traffic management being a man with a red flag! Thankfully, the crossing is now fully controlled with automatic half barriers and 'wig-wag' signals. At the time of writing the freight workings are set to continue, with a brand new fleet of bogie tanks delivered in December 2010 to replace the ageing 'TEA' tankers, the newest of which was four decades old at the time of withdrawal.

The Ribble Steam Railway also has plans to extend the line westwards for a mile and a half to meet with the Lancaster Canal's Millennium Ribble Link; if this comes to fruition it will see the operating length doubled, with the new line laid on entirely virgin ground.

The branch between Strand Road crossing and the main line at Preston has recently seen a number of diesel-hauled passenger charters work along its metals, the most notable of which occurred in 2010 when the first visit of a production series 'Deltic', in the form of 55022 Royal Scots Grey, was made to the line. To date, however, no steam-hauled passenger workings have been made over this section since its construction, but who knows what the future will hold?

**Above:** *Before long, the three Sentinel diesels were painted all-over yellow with black 'wasp stripes' added on the buffer beams. In July 1984 Energy is seen disturbing the peace of the derelict former docks site as it passes the end of Pedders Lane en route to the tar distillery situated at the west end of the dock estate. These rails have now been lifted - today the loco would coming out of the McDonalds restaurant drive through!* **Martyn Hilbert.**

**Below:** *In this 1985 view, Progress shunts the yard at the oil storage depot. Following closure of the dock in 1981, this once-extensive site provided most of the traffic for the line, with six trains each way required weekly. While part of the line still exists in use by the Ribble Steam Railway, all traces of the oil depot have now been completely swept away.* **Martyn Hilbert.**

*Below: With the re-routing of the railway along the riverbank as part of the redevelopment of the dock estate, it was now on the wrong side of the dock to serve the tar distillery and oil storage depot. The solution was the provision of a combined road and rail swing bridge across the dock entrance, constructed on the narrow canal between the dock itself and the tidal basin. This is now the primary feature of the surviving line in its new incarnation as the Ribble Steam Railway, as depicted in this February 2012 view of the oldest working standard gauge steam locomotive, Furness Railway No. 20, . The new control tower, from which the bridge, level crossings and dock gates are all controlled, is visible behind the train.* **Author.**

**Above:** *In December 2010, a new fleet of tankers was delivered for use on the revitalised bitumen traffic. One of the original Preston Corporation Sentinels,* Progress, *is pictured at the Ribble Steam Railway's Preston Riverside station with the first train.*

**Below:** *The Ribble Branch had always been a purely freight-only line, and unlike many others it did not carry a single passenger railtour in the days of steam. Since the Ribble Steam Railway opened, however, a small number of diesel-hauled passenger trains have traversed the branch. Here, 'Deltic' 55 022* Royal Scots Grey *emerges from Fishergate Tunnel and gets to grips with the 1 in 29 climb up to the station.* **Both: Author.**

# RAILS TO THE FYLDE

**Above:** *The Blackpool line was extremely busy right through the steam era, and the sheer number of summer holiday specials justified the four tracks provided from Preston to Kirkham. An impression of the heavy traffic can be gained from this image of 'Black 5' 45077 and BR Standard Class 5 73046 threading their way off the Blackpool line with a special working on 14 June 1961. Preston MPD is still open, and evidence of activity in the yard can be seen to the left of the picture.* **Tony Gillett.**

**Previous page:** *A brace of Class 104 DMUs cruise past Maudland Viaduct signalbox on a crisp winter morning in early 1973. The cars visible here are parked on St. Mark's Road, and each one would be a classic today! Note the signals fitted with blanking covers, showing that they have yet to be commissioned.* **Peter Fitton.**

Today's Blackpool line began its existence serving an altogether different Lancashire resort. Opened on 16 July 1840, less than a month after the Lancaster & Preston Railway, under the auspices of the Preston & Wyre Railway & Dock Company, it was built initially to single track formation to serve the new seaside town of Fleetwood, and was expected to carry just 15,000 passengers a year.

Fleetwood was the first planned town of the Victorian era, pioneered by Sir Peter Hesketh-Fleetwood, with construction of both the buildings and the railway line beginning in 1836. Development as a port was one of the principal reasons for its existence, and once the railway was operational it provided travellers from London with the most direct route to Scotland, the trains serving its station connecting with fast steamers to Ardrossan.

In its earliest years, as discussed in Chapter 5, a journey on the Preston & Wyre line would begin at Maudlands station, which was located on the eastern side of the main line to Lancaster. Trains travelling to Fleetwood had to cross this line on the level almost at right-angles in order to continue their journey to the coast, and this situation continued for some time. A west to south curve was added in 1844 that enabled through trains from London to travel from the main Preston station onto the Fleetwood line, but local services continued to terminate at Maudlands. The line was hugely successful, carrying 20,000 passengers in its first month of operation - 25% more than was forecast for its first full year - and was widened to double track formation in 1846. Three years after the 1847 transformation of the Preston & Wyre Railway into the Fleetwood, Preston & West Riding Junction Railway, as revealed in the previous chapter, the Maudlands terminus was abandoned in favour of an end-on connection with the Longridge branch and was replaced by the similarly-named Maudland Bridge station in 1856. This situation lasted only until the completion of the remodelling of Preston station and its northern approaches in 1885, when the present arrangement of lines was created.

**Above:** *An early view of preservation as Gresley A3 pacific 4472 Flying Scotsman comes around Maudland Curve into the Preston station environs on a bright and sunny 9 July 1967. While steam was very much still active in the area at this time, the same could not be said of Preston MPD, which had been closed and demolished. The remains of the shed floor and filled-in inspection pits can be seen in the foreground.* **Tony Gillett.**

**Below:** *The Class 45 and 46 'Peaks' were infrequent visitors to Preston, although they did appear from time to time on holiday specials to the seaside from Leeds and York, also occasionally taking over from electric motive power at Preston. 45 107 is seen at the head of a Blackpool to Euston working on 2 November 1985.* **Mick Langton.**

**Above:** *A true reflection of the early BR blue era, in the days when express trains still ran to Blackpool using prime motive power! Class 50 443 heads a Blackpool to Euston working off the viaduct at Maudlands on a crisp morning in the winter of 1972. By this tme, the signalbox was on borrowed time, and would close on 5 February 1973 with the implementation of Preston Power Box Stage 7 commissioning.*

**Below:** *Another view of Maudland Viaduct signalbox, this time from the opposite side of the line, dating from around the same time. The condition of the structure is clearly deteriorating as Class 50 434 sweeps by with a Blackpool to Euston working.*
**Both: Peter Fitton**

Beginning our journey to the coast from Preston, passing beneath Fishergate the lines are shared with the Anglo-Scottish expresses for a short distance. Prior to the remodelling, Nos. 4 and 5 signalboxes would be passed, followed by Preston's Motive Power Depot that burned down in June 1960, closed in 1961 and was demolished in 1965; as mentioned in Chapter 4 the site of the latter is now home to Preston Power Box. Immediately north of this structure, the Preston & Wyre line branches off to the north west, passing beneath the imposing bulk of St. Walburge's church on the opposite side to the West Coast Main Line and beneath Ashton Street. The route then runs alongside St. Mark's Road in a brick-lined cutting; in steam days this was a popular vantage point for spotters. With the opening of the Blackpool lines and the surge in holiday traffic in the later Victorian period, the section of the route between Maudland and Kirkham was quadrupled in 1885. This upgrade was reversed in 1965 in the wake of the Beeching Report.

At this point the surrounding land drops sharply away on either side, and Maudland Viaduct carries the line across Water Lane, Blanche Street, Pechell Street, Wyre Street and Cannon Hill. The work undertaken to this impressive structure in order to accommodate the 1885 widening can clearly be seen to this day, a track width being constructed on each side from blue engineering bricks, contrasting with the terracotta colour of the original. Having crossed the viaduct and continuing westwards, Tulketh Brow rises to the north side of the line until it is running at track level. A new link road was built here in the 1980s; today known as Tom Benson Way after the Preston-born marathon walker, it occupies the redundant trackbed of the northernmost pair of lines for around three-quarters of a mile from a point shortly before the bridge beneath Blackpool Road.

After passing below this bridge, the line is still significantly higher than much of the surrounding land, and crosses over Cottam Lane by means of a low bridge. A quarter of a mile further to the north west, Savick Brook is crossed on a single arch bridge. The route of the brook at this point is today used by the new Lancaster Canal Millennium Ribble Link to pass beneath the railway; considerable ingenuity was required to accommodate both waterway and towpath beneath the existing narrow span; the path has had to take the form of a metal walkway suspended from the bridge well above the level of the water.

**Below:** *The modern equivalent is not so majestic! On the shortest day of the year, 21 December 2010, Class 180 'Adelante' DMU 180 106 growls onto Maudland Viaduct towards Blackpool with an empty stock working from Preston to Blackpool; prior to this it had formed the 09:32 Hazel Grove to Preston service.* **Martyn Hilbert**

*A Class 110 'Calder Valley' 3-car DMU passes the block post at Ashton on its last day in use, 5 February 1973, with a Blackpool North - Leeds working. The structure was situated on the edge of the embankment at the southwest corner of Haslam Park, adjacent to the bridge over Cottam Lane, the parapets of which can just be discerned here.* **Peter Fitton.**

It is at this point that the railway and new road part company, the road turning north while the line curves west to skirt the suburbs of Cottam and Lea. Three-quarters of a mile from Savick Brook the first station on the route, Lea Road, stood on the embankment above the highway of the same name. It opened in 1842 but, partially due to the rural nature of its surroundings, never generated much traffic and was closed by the LMS on 2 May 1938. The buildings lingered on in remarkably good condition for many years, eventually being demolished in the early 1960s; virtually all traces of it have now vanished.

Continuing the journey westwards, before passing beneath Darkinson Lane the line briefly comes within sight of the Lancaster Canal then once more enters a cutting. Around a mile west of the site of Lea Road station stood the water troughs bearing the same name; confusingly, however, they were actually much closer to Lea Lane overbridge! A little further along, just over five miles from Preston, lies Salwick station; this was provided at the same time as Lea Road and was similar in design, the main difference being that the access from Station Road is from an overbridge. Like Lea Road, its surroundings are very rural and it too was closed on 2 May 1938. However, its fortunes were significantly better and it was reopened on 8 April 1940 to serve the Springfields plant (now a nuclear works) located immediately south east of the site - a purpose that continues to see it provided with a skeleton service at peak hours today.

Beyond Salwick, the line runs through the pleasant rural surroundings of Treales, passing beneath Spen Lane and Carr Lane overbridges and a brace of footbridges en route. Beyond Carr Lane the line enters the outskirts of Wesham, immediately after which Kirkham & Wesham station is reached, a little over two and a half miles from Salwick. A station, known simply as 'Kirkham', was provided on the west side of Station Road when the line opened in 1840; the present site is on the Preston side of the road and dates from 1890. Originally, a glass and iron canopy was provided to give protection to waiting passengers. This was removed in the 1960s, and today's equivalent is the common paltry 'bus shelter'!

We will cease our journey at Kirkham, as this is today's effective boundary of the Preston environs; however before doing so it is worth a look at the impact the development of the resort of Blackpool had on the line. The first route to this most popular of Lancashire seaside resorts opened in 1846, and branched off the Fleetwood line at Poulton-le-Fylde to terminate at Talbot Road, with an intermediate station at Layton opened in 1867 (originally named Bispham until 1938).

**Above:** *Stanier 'Black 5' 44692 thunders through Ashton on the fast line with a 10-coach summer holiday working from East Lancashire to Blackpool on 3 June 1960. Ashton signalbox is situated immediately behind the last coach of the train.*

**Below:** *The diesels take over. One of the first batch of English Electric Type 3s (Class 37s), D6702, accelerates through Cottam across Savick Brook with a train for Blackpool in August 1966. By this time, Blackpool Central had closed and services were but a shadow of what they had been only a couple of years previously. This bridge today carries the line over the Lancaster Canal Millennium Ribble Link.* **Both: Tony Gillett.**

*A push-pull equipment fitted Riddles BR Standard Class 2 2-6-2T, 84016, passes Cottam with a train for Fleetwood on 8 July 1961. The three-coach rake is a mixed bag of ex-LMS Period II and III vehicles, with the first two being non-corridor stock common on suburban services throughout Lancashire at the time. The land to the left of the line here is today occupied by the Preston Sports Arena.* **Tony Gillett.**

Due to the popularity of the swiftly-growing resort, Talbot Road station was rebuilt and significantly enlarged in 1898, later becoming known as Blackpool North. Six platforms were provided for normal year-round traffic; these were partially covered by an overall roof to offer passengers some protection from the weather. A further ten platforms were used for excursion traffic, which had their own entrance on Queen Street and were in essence a separate station. As they were intended only for summer use, no weather protection was provided. The station was recommended for closure in the Beeching Report, but lobbying by Blackpool Corporation saw it survive. The original station was closed and demolished in 1974, with today's facilities using eight of the former excursion platforms.

Kirkham was the junction of the Fylde Coast line to Blackpool Central (originally known as Hounds Hill until 1878) via Lytham. A short single track branch to Lytham (Station Road) was initially opened in 1846, with intermediate stations at Wrea Green (closed 1961) and Moss Side (originally called Kirkham Road, also closed in 1961 but reopened in 1983). A line from Blackpool (Hounds Hill) to Lytham (Ballam Road) was opened in 1863, and the two were finally linked together in 1874. Lytham (Station Road) station was closed at this time, leaving Ballam Road in use to the present day.

Blackpool Central was the largest and busiest of all stations in the resort, having been rebuilt to have 14 platforms in 1901. To speed up travel time by avoiding the circuitous route around the Fylde Coast line, a new direct link from Kirkham to Blackpool South was opened in 1903. Known as the Marton Line, its alignment diverged from the Preston & Wyre line at Kirkham, a flyover being provided so that up trains would not be delayed in crossing the route to Poulton. Despite the obvious convenience and other advantages of the direct line and ideal location of Blackpool Central station, Blackpool Corporation took the decision that the Marton Line and the site of Central station were ideal for redevelopment. As a result, the latter were closed in 1964, leaving the far less convenient line to Blackpool North as the main route to the resort. The route of the direct line has now been swallowed up by the M55 motorway and A5230 Yeadon Way, a less than ideal alternative to a fast and reliable train service! The Fylde Coast line has survived, albeit curtailed at Blackpool South station and provided with a less than satisfactory train service.

The line from Poulton to Fleetwood finally closed to passengers in 1970, though the route had been truncated at Fleetwood (Wyre Dock) in 1966. The track survived to serve the power station and ICI works, but both of these closed in the 1990s and the route is now mothballed. However, the Poulton & Wyre Railway Society is working to reopen the line to passengers, with the goal of providing both commuter and heritage services. With traffic on the severely congested A585 trunk road to Fleetwood growing heavier each year, perhaps a rail link to the town will once more become a viable proposition.

**Above:** *Lea Road may have lost its station in 1938 but its signalbox continued to be important. When the second structure, dating from 1889 was deemed life-expired in 1954, it was replaced by a secondhand Midland Railway Type 4a 'box, which looked decidedly out of place on the former LYR line! Lea Road 'box finally closed on 28 June 1970.* **Tony Gillett.**

**Below:** *Just under a mile west of the site of the long-closed Lea Road station lay the water troughs bearing the same name. Viewed from the vantage point of Lea Lane overbridge, 'Black 5' 44822 heads 'light engine' from Blackpool to Preston in July 1965.* **Ron Fisher.**

**Above:** *In a somewhat daring shot from track level - the photographer risking a considerable soaking from the passing train - a Riddles WD 2-8-0 90720 is pictured Blackpool-bound with a lengthy mixed freight at Lea Road troughs on 6 January 1961. The boards protecting the ballast can clearly be seen here.*

**Below:** *It wasn't just steam locomotives that benefitted from the provision of water troughs. As English Electric Type 4 (Class 40) D325 illustrates as it thunders eastwards beneath Lea Lane with a London-bound express on 6 January 1961, the early diesels were also able to top up their train heating boilers.* **Both: Tony Gillett.**

**Above:** *Class 142 'Pacer' DMU 142 064 was still carrying its original Provincial Services powder blue livery when this picture was taken, albeit with the short-lived 'Network NorthWest' logo emblazoned on the bodyside just behind the leading doors. The unit prepares to call at Salwick station with a working from Colne to Blackpool South in May 1996. Visible in the background is Salwick No. 2 signalbox, which survives to control access to the Springfields nuclear works sidings.*

**Below:** *During the period when ongoing problems with the Class 142s forced the re-introduction of some locomotive-hauled trains in Lancashire and Greater Manchester, Class 31 31 448 was working a Saturday afternoon service from Manchester Victoria to Blackpool North on 18 June 1988. The service was one of the few trains to call at Salwick Station, which at this time still retained its LYR platform canopy; sadly this has now been removed.* **Both: Martyn Hilbert.**

**Above:** *This view, taken on 2 January 1966, depicts the scene approaching Kirkham in the wake of the closure of the direct 'Marton line' to Blackpool Central. With no need for the two additional tracks from November 1964, the opportunity was taken to realign the remaining up and down lines where necessary between Kirkham and Preston.* **Tony Gillett.**

**Below:** *Regional Railways-liveried English Electric Type 3 (Class 37) 37 429 Eisteddfod Genediaethol takes the station avoiding line at Kirkham North Junction with the 13:20 Blackpool North to Liverpool Lime Street service on 14 May 1994. The ex-LYR signalbox was a place of intense activity in days gone by when all traffic to and from Blackpool South, Central & North stations, as well as Fleetwood, was controlled from here.* **Martyn Hilbert.**

# EAST LANCASHIRE AND LIVERPOOL

**Above:** *On 30 September 1961, an interloper travelled over the ELR Preston Extension. World speed record holder, Gresley A4 class 60022* Mallard *worked from Retford on the East Coast Main Line to Blackpool, in charge of a Northern Rubber Company outing. The company's chairman was a certain Mr. Alan Pegler, who had specially organised the motive power for the trip. The return leg from Blackpool was piloted by Midland Compound 4-4-0 1000. The unusual sight of an East Coast 'Streak' passing beneath Vicars Bridge was captured from the end of platforms 10 & 11.* **Peter Rigby.**

**Previous page:** *Lostock Hall is famous among enthusiasts today for its engine shed, which was the last to prepare steam locomotives for ordinary service in August 1968. Even before then its proximity to the shed made it a haven for spotters, as depicted in this 17 August 1965 view of Stanier 'Jubilee' 45698* Mars *passing through with the 12:27 Liverpool Exchange to Blackpool North.* **Peter Fitton.**

The Blackburn & Preston Railway appeared on the scene in 1846, threading its way in from the east to form a north-facing junction with the North Union Railway by means of a very sharp curve immediately south of Farington station. Shortly after the line's opening that year, it was taken over by the East Lancashire Railway (ELR), which was also in the process of acquiring the Liverpool, Ormskirk & Preston Railway Company. Construction of the latter route had not started at the time, but was completed in 1849, a bridge over the North Union Railway linking the two lines. A west to north junction was not provided, however, and trains from Liverpool to Preston had to run onto the Blackburn line as far as Lostock Hall, then reverse to run onto the North Union and complete their journey. At the time, tolls for using the short section of the West Coast Main Line between Farington Junction and Preston were hefty, adding yet another problem for the ELR.

This unsatisfactory situation lasted for around a year, until the ELR's Preston Extension was completed. This diverged from the Blackburn line at a junction between Lostock Hall and Bamber Bridge stations, running largely on embankments apart from a short length of cutting near Todd Lane, until it reached the valley of the River Ribble. This was crossed by means of a 52-arch viaduct, though the instability of the surrounding ground saw the majority of the arches quickly filled in! The river itself was spanned on three ornate cast iron arches, the viaduct being approximately mid-way between the existing North Union and Lancaster Canal Tramroad's structures in a location where an application by the Blackburn & Preston Company for a railway route had previously been refused by Preston Corporation. It was approved after the ELR agreed to incorporate a public footway within its river crossing and formally landscape the area north of the river between the Preston Extension embankment and the North Union; the latter became today's Miller Park. The embankment continued northwards, the line crossing one of the parkland roadways over a superb stone-built balustraded bridge, locally known as Ivy Bridge. After this point, the ground rose sharply on either side, the line becoming enveloped by the stone-built cutting supporting East Cliff immediately prior to entering the Preston station environs.

**Above:** *A circa 1969 view from track level on the other side of Vicars Bridge, taken from the vantage point of Ivy Bridge, shows the approaches to the East Lancashire side of the station. Preston (East Lancs. Goods) signalbox can be seen to the right immediately below the bridge.* **Martin Nield.**

**Below:** *The ornate structure of Ivy Bridge is seen to good effect in this view of an unidentified Aspinall saddle tank pausing between its shunting duties on a sunny summer day in the early 1950s. The vantage point is the main pathway through Miller Park; Avenham Park is visible through the arch.* **Ben Brooksbank.**

**Above:** *A rare colour view of the stretch between the end of the Preston Extension viaduct over the Ribble and Preston (East Lancs. Goods) signalbox, showing the proximity of the river to the station environs. The point connecting the headshunt for the Butler Street goods yard can be seen to the right of the picture, while the western parapet of Ivy Bridge is immediately in front of the left-hand corner of the signalbox.* **Peter Rigby.**

**Below:** *With only a couple of days to go before the closure of the line to Southport, Stanier 'Black 5' 45200 takes charge of the three coaches of the 15:04 Preston - Southport across the River Ribble on the ELR Preston Extension viaduct on 4 September 1964.* **Peter Fitton.**

*Looking south from the pedestrian walkway on the deck of the viaduct over the Ribble, Lostock Hall gasworks can be seen on the skyline above the rear coach of the receding train. A wealth of detail is visible, from the spiked timber rails intended to deter would-be trespassers, to the high-level rails on the bridge parapet to prevent anyone falling from a vehicle from plummeting into the river below! While this picture is undated, the empty doll on the signal at the end of the viaduct indicates that it must have been taken after September 1964 as the West Lancashire line is closed.* **Peter Rigby.**

Elsewhere on the route, further improvements were in the offing. A new station, Preston Junction, was provided on the Preston side of Todd Lane in 1852 to allow passengers from East Lancashire a cross-platform interchange into trains from Preston to Liverpool. Its name often confused passengers, and was eventually changed to Todd Lane Junction a century after its opening.

The Lancashire & Yorkshire Railway (LYR) took over the ELR in 1859, and with the construction of the new joint station in Preston the relationship with the North Union grew considerably better. By the time the latter had been succeeded by the London & North Western Railway in 1889, the LYR had plans to improve access to the station for Liverpool - Blackpool trains. These bore fruit in 1891 with the opening of the short length of line from Moss Lane Junction on the Liverpool line (named after a road that is today just a farm track leading from Bee Lane), shortly before it crossed the West Coast Main Line, to Farington Curve Junction on the latter route, located immediately below Bee Lane bridge. Trains to and from Liverpool could now run through the west side of Preston station, eliminating the need for them to cross several running lines from the East Lancashire side in order to take the Blackpool line. Things were further improved with the addition of a sharp curve linking the new Farington Curve spur with the line towards Lostock Hall opened in 1908; this benefitted trains travelling between East Lancashire and Blackpool as they no longer had to cross the main line on the level.

We now begin our journey to East Lancashire and Liverpool. Half a century ago, this would have been via the Extension line from the eastern side of Preston station. Though considered a branch line by many, it should not be forgotten that it was part of the LYR main line and was extremely busy in the days of steam. Departing the station towards Vicars Bridge, there would often be an array of coaching stock stored in the yard. Butler Street goods yard was extremely busy throughout the 1950s and early 1960s, and the view from the windows of passing trains was always one of a mass of great activity.

After passing beneath Vicars Bridge, Preston (East Lancs. Goods) signalbox could be glimpsed on the left. At this point, the route consisted of three tracks; the up and down lines and a long headshunt for Butler Street yard. In the days of steam, a 'Jinty' 0-6-0 tank locomotive could often be seen in this area, fussing around with a handful of wagons. A little further along lay the aforementioned Ivy Bridge, at which point the line passed the park keeper's cottage in Avenham Park.

**Above:** *Southport shed's Stanier 2-6-4T 42675 crosses the River Ribble viaduct and slows for Whitehouse North Junction, before veering right towards Southport with the 18:24 service from Preston on 17 August 1964. The signal seen here is the same one illustrated in the previous view, this time with all its arms intact! Note the 10mph speed restriction over the viaduct.*

**Below:** *The end has arrived for Whitehouse North Junction signalbox on 20 April 1965. This ex-LYR box (along with that at Whitehouse West Junction, both dating from 1900) became redundant with the closure of the Southport line from 7 September 1964; surprisingly, however, traces of both structures can still be found today.* **Both: Alan Castle.**

*Stanier 'Jubilee' 4-6-0 45694* Bellerophon *heads a Blackpool to Heckmondwike special away from Preston on 15 May 1964. The train is in the middle of the stretch of the ELR Preston Extension that is enclosed by the Whitehouse triangle; the roof of Whitehouse North Junction signalbox can be discerned above the train.* **Arthur Haymes.**

The embankment beyond here grew in height substantially over the next quarter of a mile until the viaduct over the Ribble was reached. At this point, the yard headshunt ended, leaving just a pair of tracks across the river. The attractive cast iron spans of 1850 were replaced by the LMS in 1930 with a somewhat utilitarian steel girder design that has stood the test of time and survives today. As with the original structure, a public walkway was perpetuated in the new construction, with the steps on the south bank of the river modified slightly. For some inexplicable reason, these were entirely removed by Lancashire County Council after the line's closure and a steep ramp hewn into the original eastern embankment as a replacement.

Beyond the river the line continued on the former 52-arch viaduct, by now filled in to form an embankment; this stretch was almost a quarter of a mile long and its extent can be identified today by the exposed coping stones that are occasionally visible on the western side of the trackbed. Originally, Whitehouse North Junction signalbox was located at the end of the former viaduct, provided to control access between the West Lancashire Line and Preston station. This closed in 1964 and, being of all-timber construction, was quickly disposed of the following year. Part of the floor of the building can still be seen dumped on the western side of the embankment – opposite the point in which it was originally located. The Whitehouse Junction triangle could be glimpsed to the right from an outbound train, the south side finally rejoining the Extension line by Whitehouse South Junction signalbox, positioned 600 yards from the structure at North Junction immediately before Factory Lane underbridge. All traces of this 'box have now been swept away due to the unwarranted demolition of a number of the bridges on the line by Lancashire County Council in the early 1990s and the battering back of the embankment to remove the bridge piers.

The land between the river and Factory Lane is mainly rural in nature, even today being used as pasture for grazing cattle. However, as its name suggests the land on the western side of the line to the south of Factory Lane was given over to industrial use. Vernon's Surgical Dressings' large Penwortham Mills site opened in 1915 giving its name to the road, and as Vernon Carus was a bustling place until the business moved to new premises in 2006. The impressive buildings are now being demolished to make way for yet another vast and unnecessary housing development. The land south of Penwortham Mills was given over to Lostock Hall gasworks; its construction began in 1925 and by the 1950s it sprawled over more than 40 acres. A dedicated fan of sidings was provided, accessed off the Extension line, to which coal was delivered twice daily (except on Mondays, when only one delivery was made, and the Sunday workings were discontinued in the 1960s), and from which the chemical by-products were taken away. The gasworks had its own steam locomotive, which in the 1950s and 60s was a Peckett 0-4-0 saddle tank (Works No. 1820), to move the wagons around the works. Train services to the sidings eventually ceased in 1977, and much of the site has now been cleared and given over to housing.

**Above:** *The photographer has used the vantage point of the bridge over Factory Lane to capture this view of Stanier 'Jubilee' 45589 Gwalior passing Whitehouse South Junction signalbox with the Saturdays-only Blackpool Central to Castleford on 8 August 1964. The massive bulk of Lostock Hall gasworks dominates the skyline.*

**Below:** *On the same date as the picture above, another 'Jubilee' - 45694 Bellerophon again, leaves Whitehouse South towards Todd Lane Junction. The train is alongside the Penwortham Mill of Vernon's Surgical Dressings.* **Both: Peter Fitton.**

**Above:** *A busy scene at Todd Lane Junction (originally Preston Junction) at 09:54 on 31 August 1965 as Riddles BR Standard Class 4 4-6-0 75033 drifts in on a Preston to Liverpool Exchange service, passing Stanier 'Black 5' 45196 on a Colne to Blackpool North working. By this time, trains to Southport had ceased and the majority of the holiday specials had gone, depriving the route of much of its through traffic.* **Peter Fitton.**

Immediately beyond the gasworks sidings, the line crossed the end of Wateringpool Lane before passing once more through a small area of open farmland, though much of this has been swallowed up by housing since the early 1960s. Just under two miles from Preston, and still in the shadow of the gasworks, Todd Lane Junction station was reached. Despite the industry situated immediately to the north, its location was pleasantly rural and its proximity to the Brownedge area of Lostock Hall supplied it with adequate passengers to justify its existence. The station took the form of an island platform, accessed via steps from the bridge that carried Todd Lane North over the line, and stood in a shallow cutting, its buildings and central platform area protected by a canopy supported on cast iron pillars. 'Parachute' water columns were located within the cutting slopes at either end of the platforms, and a short bay, originally constructed to hold a spare locomotive, was let into the south end of the platform on the west side, immediately below the bridge. Though the station closed in 1969, being outlasted by the Extension line by three years, the platform survived intact until the early 1990s when Lancashire County Council took the inexplicable action of removing every trace of it. A pond now occupies the site.

Passing beneath the bridge, Todd Lane Junction signalbox stood immediately on the left, after which the junction itself provided a choice of routes; the right-hand fork took trains around the sharp curve towards Lostock Hall, beneath Brownedge Road to join the route to Liverpool. The remaining pair of lines proceeded straight ahead to cross Brownedge Road by means of a level crossing, finally curving to the left to join the main East Lancashire line to Blackburn and beyond just before Bamber Bridge station. The Preston Extension was closed in 1972, apart from the short section to the gasworks sidings which lasted for a further five years. The traffic is now concentrated on the increasingly congested West Coast Main Line as far as Farington Curve Junction where the routes to Liverpool and Blackburn diverge today. With so few paths available for trains on the busy main line, there are very limited opportunities for service improvements on the former East Lancashire lines; sadly, the reopening of the Extension line is not a viable option due to the construction of the A6 London Way, which bisects the route on the level shortly before Brownedge crossing.

*How things changed in a few short years! By May 1968, Todd Lane Junction station was in decline. While it was still open at this time, its appearance was one of dereliction; the canopy was falling apart and weeds were taking over the once-pristine flower beds. The short bay, 'parachute' water columns and the bottom of the access steps are seen to good effect in this view taken from Todd Lane North overbridge. After closure, the buildings were demolished but the platform survived in situ until the early 1990s.* **Ivan Stewart.**

We will therefore resume our modern-day journey towards Blackburn at Farington Curve Junction. The line branches off the West Coast Main Line here to the west, with the route to Liverpool forking off to the right immediately afterwards. The Blackburn line climbs sharply, curving round to the east. In steam days, shortly before crossing over the main line on a bridge at Farington, it joined the direct line from Liverpool at Lostock Hall Engine Shed Junction. An arch bridge carries the track over Croston Road, after which Lostock Hall motive power depot could be seen on the right. This was the last shed in Britain to prepare steam locomotives for ordinary passenger trains in August 1968; it lingered on as a carriage and wagon repair shed and cripple sidings for a further two decades, finally being entirely demolished in 1990. The site today is completely derelict and overgrown, though the areas once occupied by the inspection pits, coaling stage and turntable can still be identified by a keen observer.

Lostock Hall station was located alongside the engine shed site, on the west side of Watkin Lane, a little under three miles from Preston. It was a modest two-platform affair equipped with timber buildings by the LYR, but closed on 7 August 1968. Due to public pressure, a new halt was provided in September 1984, sited on the other side of Watkin Lane overbridge to the original. The facilities are meagre even by modern standards but it generates a healthy amount of passenger traffic for the hourly services to Preston or to Blackburn and Colne, which are the only trains to call there. The goods yard and carriage sidings once occupied the land immediately south east of the present halt. A stone-built goods shed, a coal yard and various huts were dotted around the site, though all have since been swept away. Moving further east, Lostock Hall Junction is reached; this is the point where the link from Farington Junction on the West Coast Main Line joins, coming in from the south west, and until 1977 was also where the line towards Todd Lane Junction diverged to the north east. Today, the area between the junction and the point where the A6 London Way crosses the track is flooded with modern housing. After passing beneath the dual carriageway, Bamber Bridge football club can be glimpsed on the left, with the former connection from Todd Lane Junction – today lingering on in a derelict state as a siding – curving in beyond it, joining the through line at Bamber Bridge Junction. To the right is the yard of Bowker Haulage with a rail connection that survives today, albeit little used.

**Above:** *Trains taking the right-hand fork at Todd Lane Junction would curve westwards, passing beneath Brownedge Road to emerge on the Liverpool line at Lostock Hall Junction. English Electric Type 4 (Class 40) 250 is doing just this on 8 July 1972 while in charge of a Blackpool North to Newcastle working during the remodelling of Preston station. After travelling through Lostock Hall, the train would curve north to rejoin the main line at Farington Curve Junction and pass through Preston station again on its way to Carlisle. Within a few short weeks, this once-regular turning manoeuvre would no longer be possible.*
***Peter Fitton.***

**Below:** *Another view of Lostock Hall station, this time from the Blackburn-bound platform, as Stanier 'Jubilee' 45666 Cornwallis drifts to a stop with a Liverpool to Preston train on 12 March 1965. The passengers' bad habit of 'opening the door before the train has come to a complete stand' is apparent here!* ***Tony Gillett.***

*Trains taking the left-hand fork at Todd Lane would emerge on the Liverpool to Blackburn line immediately west of Bamber Bridge station. A Cravens Class 105 power twin DMU (locally known as 'Accrington sets') pauses at the station on 23 August 1980 with a Preston to Colne working. Note the unusual flat-roofed signalbox, which survives in use to this day to supervise the level crossing visble here.* **Martyn Hilbert.**

Immediately beyond the junction lies Bamber Bridge station, which was opened with the line in 1846 and has survived remarkably intact when compared with many others on the line. The station has been unmanned since 1969 and the buildings on the Blackburn-bound platform were demolished in the 1970s; however, those on the westbound side have survived. They have recently been refurbished and are in use as a pensioners' drop-in centre at the time of writing. At the east end of the platforms, the level crossing over Station Road was the bane of the motorist's existence in the days before the M6 Preston Bypass was opened. It is still in use today, albeit with lifting barriers and wig-wag signals in place of the original gates. Until recently, there was a glass-roofed subway that allowed passengers to cross beneath the line without being restricted by the movement of passing trains; this has now been removed and no trace remains.

The signalbox here survives to control the Station Road level crossing, along with two others to the east via CCTV links. Beyond this point the line passes beneath the M6 motorway before running alongside Walton Summit industrial estate; Brindle Road level crossing is located at the western end of the latter, alongside the Hospital Inn. A little beyond this point, the railway passes beneath the M61 Preston to Manchester motorway, which opened in 1969, emerging on the other side into unspoiled countryside with open aspects on either side. A further level crossing is encountered at Gregson Lane, after which the line reaches the edge of the village of Hoghton.

Hoghton itself was once home to a quaint country station, provided from the opening of the East Lancashire line in 1846. Small buildings stood on each of the two platfoms, which were all built of stone from the local quarry behind nearby Hoghton Tower. An iron lattice footbridge linked the platforms, and a level crossing stood at the eastern end of the station. This inconvenience to the road user was largely overcome in the early 1930s with the construction of a by-pass and overbridge a few hundred yards to the east. A small goods yard was located to the north of the station, with a few sidings and a hand crane to aid the unloading of goods. Hoghton station closed to passengers in September 1960, the goods facilities disappearing two years later; no trace of it remains today. The signalbox, which stood on the opposite side of Station Road to the crossing, survived for some time; when its signalling use was made obsolete with the commissioning of Preston Power Box in 1973, it remained in place to work the crossing until this was placed under automatic control in 1976. In BR days, it marked the eastern fringe of the Preston area, and thus is a convenient place to break our journey for a look at the Liverpool line.

*A brace of Cravens 'Accrington sets' in original green livery with yellow warning panels passes through the closed Hoghton station with a Preston to Skipton service, circa 1964. All traces of the station have now vanished.* **Peter Fitton**

Leaving the main line at Farington Curve Junction, the line to Ormskirk and Liverpool branches off to the right of the route to Lostock Hall. Today, the line is single track throughout, with a solitary passing loop at Rufford, and is truncated at Ormskirk. The resulting impression gained by many passengers is one of a sleepy little branch line; however, this was far from the case until recently. In the dying days of steam the route was still used by fast Anglo-Scottish expresses, and its straight alignment and gentle gradients meant that even 'Black 5s' reached the magic speed of 100mph on occasion, when in the hands of the best enginemen determined to show that steam could still 'do its stuff'!

Heading away along the Farington Connecting Line, the railway immediately passes beneath Flag Lane bridge; though still parallel to the Blackburn line here, from this point onwards the route to Ormskirk enters a separate cutting before running under Coote Lane and Church Lane. Beyond, the ground levels out and the railway begins to climb above it on an embankment. The level crossing at Lodge Lane is reached next; this road was once called Moss Lane and gave its name to the junction with the Blackburn line, which ran in from the east at this point. Next to be crossed is the A582 Penwortham Way, constructed in the 1980s to bypass Lostock Hall; the route taken by the road is so roundabout that most traffic still tears through the residential areas instead! By the time the road opened, the railway had been downgraded to single track and a simple steel girder bridge carries it high above the tarmac.

The surrounding fields reach track level once more forming a largely flat, marshy plain stretching out into the distance. A quick succession of occupation crossings take Brook Lane, Naptha Lane and Parker Lane over the line before it curves to the south west; after straightening out, the interestingly-named Sod Hall Lane is crossed on the level. Until October 1961, Midge Hall station and goods yard would have been the next reached. This was opened by the LYR in 1859 but never generated much passenger traffic, principally due to its very rural location; its pre-Beeching closure can therefore be understood. Surprisingly, the station buildings, goods shed and platforms survive largely intact over half a century after closure, and proposals were recently mooted to provide passenger facilities here once more as a way to combat the severe traffic congestion in the area. These are unlikely to come to fruition due to the high costs quoted to construct a new halt.

Immediately after passing through Midge Hall's platforms, a barrier-operated crossing controls the line's passage over Midge Hall Lane. The signalbox here also survives to supervise the halting of traffic on this fairly busy thoroughfare. Adjacent is the Midge Hall pub, once the Railway Hotel, another surviving relic of the early days of the line that thankfully still enjoys a brisk trade. Beyond the crossing, the railway continues its arrow-straight course across the flat plain, traversing a number of occupation crossings and running beneath an overbridge before passing under Cocker Bar Road. There was a station here, bearing the same name as the highway, from around 1850 until it was replaced by Midge Hall in 1859.

**Above:** *A great deal of freight worked into the Preston area from East Lancashire and as far afield as the Eastern Region. On 6 September 1967, Stanier 8F 48710 comes off the line from Lostock Hall at Farington Curve Junction, and is about to take its lengthy coal train onto the West Coast Main Line to Preston.* **Peter Fitton.**

**Below:** *A view of the present-day arrangements at Farington Curve Junction, taken from Bee Lane overbridge. Class 142 'Pacer' 142 035 has left the main line behind and is crossing over the lines to East Lancashire to take the junction for Ormskirk on 24 May 2012.* **Author.**

*In the days when the Liverpool line was still an important double-track express route, Riddles BR Standard Class 4 4-6-0 75047 is about to pass beneath Coote Lane overbridge, Whitestake, with a Glasgow to Liverpool Exchange working on 28 August 1965.* **Peter Fitton.**

The modern prisons of Wymott and Garth in Bretherton can be glimpsed to the south east, after which the line crosses the River Lostock on the approach to Croston. Today, the first station on the branch is located here, some eight and a half miles from Preston, immediately south west of Bretherton Road overbridge. One platform survives, albeit substantially rebuilt, and the station building is also still in situ and remains in use as a private dwelling. Passenger accommodation is now provided by the standard rudimentary 'bus shelter'.

After departing the station, the site of the brick and tile works can be seen to the west; a small industrial estate now occupies the land, while the two former clay pits beyond have been transformed into fishing lakes. On the east side of the line, Croston village has expanded to fill the gap between the railway, Station Road and the River Yarrow. The line crosses the latter by means of a girder bridge before passing beneath the A581 Meadowhouse Lane and emerging on the other side into unspoiled countryside once more. The flat, marshy land of Croston Moss is traversed on a low embankment; this ground gave considerable trouble during the construction of the line, which had to be supported on 40-foot long timber piles driven into the soil to prevent the ground simply swallowing up the imported material. From the slightly elevated position of a passing train, the skill of the Victorian engineers can be appreciated simply by looking at the waterlogged marsh on either side!

The River Douglas is crossed next, immediately after which the passing loop at Rufford commences. The station here is reached after traversing yet another level crossing; this is the only one to retain two platforms, both of which are in use at the present time. The station buildings are long gone, with only a 'bus shelter' style structure to provide weather protection on each platform - albeit of more substantial construction than the one at Croston. The signalbox too has vanished, replaced with a Portakabin on the northbound platform.

Continung towards Ormskirk, the line follows the Rufford branch of the Leeds & Liverpool Canal (more commonly known simply as the Rufford Canal), visible to the west, for a short distance. Craft can now travel between the Lancaster Canal at Preston to the Leeds & Liverpool for the first time; with the construction of the Millennium Ribble Link (see Chapter 7), a route exists via the River Ribble to the Douglas and the Rufford Canal, which joins the Leeds & Liverpool at Burscough. In what had been virgin farmland in the 1960s, a marina adjacent to Rufford station now caters for the ever-growing number of narrowboats using the waterway. The River Douglas meanders its way through the flat landscape on the eastern side before curving away towards Parbold; a little further on, the canal passes under the line and continues to follow it on the eastern side.

**Above:** *Substituting for the non-availablity of a Class 142 'Pacer' unit, a Class 108 two-car DMU returned to its old stamping ground on 16 May 1992. With car 54238 leading, the 08:21 Ormskirk to Preston Service has just returned the single-line token at Midge Hall signalbox. The unit is about to pass through the derelict platforms of the former station, closed in October 1961.*

**Below:** *A two-car Class 108 DMU passes Cocker Bar, Ulnes Walton, with a Preston to Ormskirk service on New Years Eve 1982. The distant signal is for Preston-bound trains approaching Midge Hall. The former main line was singled west of Midge Hall in 1972; all trains now use what was the former down line.* **Both: Martyn Hilbert.**

*Showing that not all first-generation BR DMUs looked the same, a Class 101 two-car unit with car 53328 at the rear departs Croston with an evening Ormskirk to Preston service on 3 September 1986.* **Martyn Hilbert.**

There are several more farm and level crossings along the stretch between Rufford and Burscough, with one of these being on the canal bridge to enable a crossing of both railway and waterway to take place simultaneously. To the west side, the A59 road from Preston to Liverpool runs parallel to the line here, with both elevated slightly above the surrounding marsh. Approaching Burscough, the railway crosses Warper's Moss Lane on an underbridge, after which was located the junction for Burscough North Curve, which allowed trains from Preston to access the line from Wigan to Southport. This was closed in 1969 and lifted in 1973, though there are plans to reinstate it to provide a much needed Preston to Southport service.

Next to be crossed is the Wigan to Southport line itself. Unlike the Preston to Ormskirk route, this survives in double-track formation, enabling the provision of a frequent train service. A pleasant stone-built underbridge carries the line above School Lane, after which the now-redundant Burscough South Curve appears on the west side. This survived longer than the North Curve; despite passenger services along it ceasing in 1962, it continued to be used by freight trains serving the Ministry of Defence depot that was located on the eastern side of the line immediately south of the junction. The track around the curve was singled in 1970, closed in 1982 and finally lifted in the mid-1980s.

Beyond the junction with the South Curve the line crosses the Leeds & Liverpool Canal, after which the site of the MoD depot has now been swamped with housing. Burscough Junction station is reached next; this has retained its name, despite the two curves being a thing of the past, in order to distinguish it from Burscough Bridge station on the Wigan to Southport line. Burscough Junction is similar to Croston, with a single waiting shelter on its only operational platform, accessed via a ramp from Junction Lane. Continuing on the final leg of our journey to Ormskirk, the line is flanked on both sides by housing; much of that to the east dates from the 1950s and would have been a feature in steam days, while that to the west was constructed in the 1970s and 80s. After passing beneath Square Lane, a mix of industrial premises and housing can be seen to the west; again, some dates back to steam days although there are many recent additions. In contrast, on the east side, land once swallowed up by quarrying is now returning to nature.

Having crossed the track known as Abbey Lane by means of a level crossing, the line enters a short stretch of open countryside to run parallel with the A59 road once more. A small modern housing estate to the west is the first sign of impending arrival in Ormskirk; this has been built on the site of an industrial unit, though a number of other factories and warehouses survive on the same side as we draw nearer to the terminus. To the east, the disused trackbed of the former route to Skelmersdale and Rainford can be seen curving towards the line in the direction of Liverpool; this was closed to passengers in 1956, with goods services withdrawn from Rainford in 1961 and from Skelmersdale two years later. Immediately beyond the former junction, Ormskirk station is reached, the terminus of the line from Preston being at a set of buffer stops installed mid-way along the surviving platform. Passengers wishing to continue their journey to Liverpool have to alight from the train that has brought them from Preston, walk along the platform and board a Merseyrail electric unit!

**Above:** *Stanier 'Black 5' 45212 thunders through the station at Croston on 14 April 1968 with the 19:50 Sundays-only Liverpool Exchange to Glasgow service. This was recognised as part of the 'racing stretch', where even everyday workhorses like the 'Black 5s' could achieve speeds of up to 100mph. The inset shows the speedometer of classmate 45444 just shy of the magic 'ton' approaching Rufford on 26 September 1967.* **Peter Fitton / Tony Gillett (inset).**

**Below:** *Today's equivalent is far less glamorous, and much slower! Class 153 'skateboard' single-car DMU 153 307 calls at a decimated Croston station on 24 March 2008 with an Ormskirk - Preston service.* **Martin Brown.**

**Above:** *Accelerating away from Croston with a Preston to Ormskirk Service on 26 September 1987, a Class 101 two-car DMU, with 53334 leading, passes over Club Lane Level Crossing. The unit is beginning to show its age, and judging by the colour of the exhaust the engines are getting a little tired! The former crossing keeper's cottage on this former double track main line is on the right of this view.*

**Below:** *With the oil seed rape in full bloom, Merseytravel-liveried Class 142 'Pacer' unit 142 057 passes Club Lane Crossing, having just departed from Croston with a Preston to Ormskirk service in May 2005.* **Both: Martyn Hilbert.**

**Above:** *Northern Rail Class 153 single-car DMU 153 330 has just left Rufford and is heading for Preston across the River Douglas on 9 April 2009. The view has been captured from the vantage point of the path that follows the eastern bank of the river; the foot crossing can be seen to the left of the picture. Immediately west of the bridge are the points at the northeast end of the passing loop.* **Martin Brown.**

**Below:** *In this mid-1980s photograph, a Class 104 DMU is held at Rufford's home signal by the passing loop while the signalman opens the crossing gates. This scene has now changed completely; the signalbox has gone and the gates have been replaced by barriers.* **Martyn Hilbert.**

**Above:** *In spring 1988, an original Provincial blue-liveried Class 142 'Pacer' enters Rufford station with a service from Preston to Ormskirk. The proximity of the platforms to the crossing can clearly be seen.* **David Fowler.**

**Below:** *Prototype Class 140 railbus 140 001 is seen at Rufford during a trial run between Ormskirk and Preston in September 1981. The narrow bodyshell of the unit is apparent when comparing this view with the one of the production series vehicles above.* **Martin Brown.**

**Above:** *In the days when there were still (just about) two tracks through Ormskirk station, Merseyrail was saying goodbye to the last of the LMS-designed electric units. The 'Class 503 Farewell' railtour was a joint effort organised by the Railway Correspondence & Travel Society and the Locomotive Club of Great Britain. The train, formed from a pair of 1938-built 3-car sets led by car M28690M, awaits its last departure from the terminus on 13 April 1985. In the background can be seen a Class 108 DMU that has terminated in the former up platform with a service from Preston; in the foreground is the old down line, then used as an emergency loop to bypass the two truncated sections of track at Ormskirk.* **Martyn Hilbert.**

**Below:** *The station today is but a shadow of its former self; only a single line now remains and is physically disconnected in the middle of the platform. Passeneger accommodation consists of a converted steel container, as seen in this view of Class 156 'Sprinter' DMU 156 468, which has just arrived with a special charter from Preston on 7 December 2008.* **Martin Brown.**

# THE WEST LANCASHIRE LINE

**Above:** *After departing Preston station's East Lancashire platforms, trains joined the line to Southport via Whitehouse North curve. With only two days to go until the line closed forever, Stanier 'Black 5' 44686 approaches Whitehouse North Junction, heading for Preston in charge of the 13:50 service from Southport on 4 September 1964. Whitehouse North Junction signalbox can be seen ahead of the locomotive.* **Peter Fitton.**

**Previous page:** *The line's rural surroundings were part of its charm, but the number of manned level crossings in remote spots meant that it was expensive to operate. One such location was Nursery Lane, on the climb away from New Longton & Hutton towards Longton Bridge.* **Alan Castle.**

Until 1882, the journey from Preston to Southport by rail was rather long and circuitous, having to be made via the line to Ormskirk and Liverpool as far as Burscough North Curve (see Chapter 8) before using the latter to join the line from Wigan to reach the seaside resort. Plans to remedy this situation were made by the West Lancashire Railway (WLR), which planned a completely independent route in order to challenge the virtual monopoly enjoyed by the Lancashire & Yorkshire Railway.

The route was promoted by various wealthy concerns in affluent Southport, and with the link to Preston being the principal concern, it was planned without much regard to generation of traffic at intermediate points. The line thus threaded a fairly direct route between the two towns, crossing vast expanses of marshy and virtually unpopulated countryside. A bill authorising the building of the line was passed in August 1871, with the cutting of the first sod ceremoniously carried out by the Lord Mayor of Southport, Alderman Samuel Swire, in the seaside town on 18 April 1873. Construction was somewhat protracted, owing to the company experiencing severe financial difficulties on several occasions. The easiest stretch of line to construct was, therefore, the first to open. With the route completed between Hesketh Park, on the outskirts of Southport, and Hesketh Bank close to the River Douglas, the first passenger trains ran on 19 February 1878. Intermediate stations along this stretch were provided (from south to north) at Churchtown, Crossens and Banks, and an impressive iron swing bridge was constructed to carry the railway over the navigable River Douglas. In July that year, an additional stop (initially without a station) was made at the level crossing by the small hamlet of Hundred End, mid-way between the villages of Banks and Hesketh Bank. Hundred End eventually gained two short platforms; these were lengthened in October 1895, and a pair of simple wooden waiting shelters were added at the same time.

The link needed to take the line into Southport was finally made on 10 June 1878 with the opening of a temporary station at Windsor Road; further extension from Hesketh Bank to the north took some time, with the rails reaching Longton station (Longton Bridge from 1892) on 18 May 1882, with an intermediate station at Hoole.

**Above:** *The Railway Correspondence & Travel Society organised the 'Ribble Lune Railtour' to run on 23 May 1964, utilising Carlisle Kingmoor-based BR Standard Class 6 pacific 72007* Clan Mackenzie. *The journey began at the East Lancashire side of Preston and proceeded along the West Lancashire line to Roe Lane Junction near Southport. Here, the train is seen on Whitehouse North Curve, with the West Junction signalbox and bridge beneath the main line in sight.*

**Below:** *Whitehouse South Curve provided trains from the Blackburn direction with a connection to the Southport line. 'Black 5' 45218, one of several of the class based at Southport shed, threads its way towards the West Junction with the 17:27 Blackburn to Southport train on 22 August 1964. This service will call at all stations except Penwortham and Hoole.* Both: ***Alan Castle.***

**Above:** *The London & North Western Railway G2a class 'Super D' 0-8-0s were not regular performers on the Southport line, but Wigan Springs Branch-based 49451 was put in charge of the Railway Correspondence & Travel Society's 'Mid-Lancs Railtour' on 22 September 1962. The train originated at the former Fishergate Hill terminus, and is seen heading from Preston across the iron girder bridge on Whitehouse North Curve.* **Tony Gillett.**

**Below:** *The fireman's view of Whitehouse West Junction signalbox from Lostock Hall's BR Standard Class 2 2-6-0 78040 heading the 13:17 Southport to Preston on the last day of the line's existence, 6 September 1964. The locomotive has just passed beneath the West Coast Main Line and is about to swing sharply to the left onto the North Curve for the final half-mile climb into Preston.* **Alan Castle.**

*Another view of 'Super D' 0-8-0 49451 on the 'Mid-Lancs Railtour' on 22 September 1962. The location this time is Penwortham Junction, and the locomotive is in the process of propelling its train onto the main line from the link leading to the original WLR terminus at Fishergate Hill. Upon departure from Preston, the train travelled up the Longridge branch.* **Peter Fitton.**

The final four and a half miles from Longton to Preston were also nearing completion, with the stone and iron viaduct across the Ribble the last piece of the puzzle to be completed; the first trains ran on 4 September that year in conjunction with the Preston Guild celebrations. The line's Preston terminus was a grand one with a 400ft island platform, half of which was covered with an ornate iron and glass overall roof with a 70ft span. The main station building was constructed in a Gothic style from local Longridge stone, and had a three-storey tower on its western elevation. On the same date as the opening of the line to Preston, the temporary Southport terminus at Windsor Road was replaced with an impressive and imposing permanent one at Derby Road, similar in design to that at Preston. The full passenger timetable on the route was finally implemented on 16 September 1882.

From the outset, the WLR was in financial difficulty. The realisation dawned that an isolated route was unlikely to be financially viable, and a number of schemes were put forward. A route from Hesketh Bank to Blackpool was promoted in 1882, though this would have required a long and expensive viaduct over the River Ribble near Freckleton. This proved to be the route's downfall, as it would have prevented the development of Preston as a port by interfering with the navigation of the river, and the plans were thus strongly opposed by Preston Corporation and consequently dropped. A marginally more successful proposal was put forward in conjunction with the Manchester, Sheffield & Lincolnshire Railway (MSLR), which at the time was seeking to expand aggressively and acquire a share in the lucrative Blackpool traffic. As part of this scheme, the MSLR put forward a route from the WLR at New Longton that would link with its own Manchester to Wigan line. Expansion towards Blackpool was to be via the Preston Dock railway, and despite the necessary parliamentary bills being applied for in 1883, none came to fruition.

Also in 1883, the WLR finally succumbed to the inevitable and a link was constructed from its line at Penwortham near Preston beneath the West Coast Main Line to the East Lancashire Railway's Preston Extension at Whitehouse (later Whitehouse South) Junction, which was by that time under the ownership of the LYR. This allowed trains from the Blackburn direction to travel to Southport (and vice versa) via the WLR. A triangular junction was provided at the western end of the line, diverging from Middleforth Junction on the link line to curve north to Ribble Junction (to reach Fishergate Hill station) or south to Penwortham Junction (towards Southport). Despite finally being connected to the wider railway network, the WLR continued to lose money and finally went into receivership in 1886. However, the trains still ran, and a number of improvements were made, including the provision of a station at Hutton, between Longton and Preston, in 1889. Despite actually managing to make a profit for the first time in 1895, it was finally taken over by the LYR two years later.

**Above:** *We take a short diversion from our journey to Southport to look at the goods-only line to the former WLR Fishergate Hill terminus. This view, taken in July 1972, more than seven years after the line serving it was closed, clearly shows the elaborate Gothic architecture of the station building. Sadly, all traces of this fine structure have now vanished.* **Peter Rigby.**

**Below:** *Fishergate Hill station survived for goods use until January 1965. By this time, while the buildings were in private use as rented office space and still in good condition, the view from the trackside was altogether different. An English Electric 350hp (Class 08) shunter, D4021, propels a rake of wagons past the derelict signalbox in the mid-1960s.* **Ivan Stewart.**

*The West Lancashire Railway went to great expense to provide a river crossing leading to its own Preston terminus. While passenger trains lasted for barely two decades, the structure survived to provide access to the goods station until its final closure. Latterly, the only working to use the line was a daily trip working from Lostock Hall that brought supplies, via the Whitehouse South curve, to the sidings of R. Silcock & Sons, a local firm of provender merchants that occupied the former station. This undated view depicts the final demolition of the bridge girders; the piers survive today.* **Alan Castle.**

Once under LYR ownership, the line received the shake-up it badly needed. The independent termini were abandoned in favour of linking the erstwhile ELR with the new owner's own stations at either end. At Preston, this simply involved constructing a new north-facing curve from Whitehouse West Junction, immediately east of the West Coast Main Line bridge on the ELR - WLR link, to join the Preston Extension at Whitehouse North junction. This was completed on 16 July 1900, and Fishergate Hill station was formally closed to passengers following the 1902 Guild, continuing in use as a goods station. The junction at Middleforth was removed in 1905, having seen little use since the opening of the new Whitehouse Curve. Things were a little more involved at the Southport end, and the LYR embarked on a major remodelling of the approaches to its Chapel Street station to accommodate a number of improvements, of which the diversion of the WLR from Derby Road into the station was but one. The Liverpool, Southport & Preston Railway had a linked the Cheshire Lines Committee route from Aintree to Southport Lord Street with the WLR via a triangular junction at Meols Cop in 1887, and trains using this route also ran into Derby Road. In May 1901, a short length of line was opened that linked the WLR with the LYR's Southport to Wigan line at St. Luke's station, where platforms were added to cater for the new route. Derby Road was temporarily closed and fell into a state of disrepair, though it was restored to use as a goods station and offices in 1913, finally closing completely in December 1973.

Hutton station had its name changed to Hutton & Howick in 1897, finally becoming New Longton & Hutton in 1924 after the village of New Longton began to spring up around the railway. In 1911, a new halt was added at Cop Lane to serve the rapidly growing town of Penwortham; initially bearing only the name of the adjacent road, this was changed to the full title of 'Penwortham Cop Lane' by the LMS in 1940.

By the turn of the 20th Century, Crossens had become a busy commuter suburb of Southport. In response to growing competition from trams and road transport at the Southport end, the LYR decided that its forthcoming electrification of the Liverpool to Southport line should be extended to Crossens. The line to Meols Cop was already to be electrified, and new electric car sheds were provided within the triangular area enclosed by the junction. The first electric services between Crossens and Liverpool via Southport ran on 6 May 1904, and proved to be highly successful. The Preston services continued to be steam-hauled throughout.

**Above:** *One of Southport's Caprotti valve geared 'Black 5s', 44745, rolls a westbound train along the last few yards into Penwortham Cop Lane station, beneath the impressive three-arch bridge that carried a farm track over the line, on 31 August 1964. This part of the route has been obliterated by the construction of the A582 Golden Way section of the Penwortham Bypass.*

**Below:** *The very last day for the station at Penwortham Cop Lane, the country station in the heart of the Preston suburbs. Lostock Hall shed's Riddles BR Standard Class 2 2-6-0 78041 was in charge of a number of services on 6 September 1964, and was touchingly adorned with an appropriate 'Last Day' headboard. Its arrival at the head of the 14:34 Preston to Southport train has attracted more than the usual number of admirers (on both platforms).* **Both: Alan Castle.**

*The scene overlooking the station site from Cop Lane bridge on 16 January 1965, only 19 weeks after the passage of the last train. Due to the high fire risk from the all-timber construction, the obliteration of this station preceded that of all others on the line.* **Alan Castle.**

The West Lancashire line handled a wide variety of goods. The fertile ground surrounding the line between Longton Bridge and Crossens was already a busy market garden growing district when the railway came on the scene; this rapidly expanded in the early years of the 20th Century and continues to this day. Thus, the transport of fruit, vegetables and flowers provided a fair amount of traffic along the route. Hesketh Park was the nearest railway coal yard to Southport's northern suburbs, while milk traffic to the district from further afield was also plentiful; the marshy ground, while ideal for growing purposes, was far less ideal for grazing cattle.

Busy it may have been, but the number of gated level crossings, overstaffed stations and signalling block posts along the sparsely-populated route, together with the use of large locomotives on short trains in later years, meant that as road competition increased the line was unable to pay its way. While other lines were being modernised with automatic crossings, colour light signalling and the use of diesel multiple units, the West Lancashire line lingered on in the steam age. All stations on the original route east of Banks retained their traditional pre-war LMS wooden signage and oil or gas lighting. When Beeching short-sightedly wielded his axe, the line was a prime candidate for early closure. Despite protests, the sad day finally came on Sunday 6 September 1964, the line closing with effect from the following day - surprisingly, this also included the electrified section from Crossens. Electric services from Crossens had ceased on the previous day, there being no timetabled electric trains on a Sunday. Track lifting and demolition began in January 1965.

Preston Fishergate Hill goods station remained open until January 1965, while a single line survived from Southport as far as Hesketh Park to serve the coal yard, which lasted until November 1967; the last vestiges of the line were gone by the end of the following year. Today, the replacement bus journey is long, unreliable and severely affected by the heavy traffic congestion that swamps the parallel roads and all approaches to both Preston and Southport. Of all the routes in the north west of England that have closed in the wake of the Beeching Report, the West Lancashire line is the one most in need of reinstatement. While a number of plans have been proposed to reopen it and over 80% is intact today, a number of housing developments have sprung up on most of the station sites and it is therefore likely that the line is sadly forever consigned to the history books.

*On the balmy summer morning of 9 August 1964, a shabby 42286, one of Lostock Hall's fleet of Fairburn 2-6-4 tank engines, clears its cylinders following departure from Penwortham Cop Lane on its way to the seaside with the 10:12 working from Preston.* **Alan Castle.**

Beginning our steam-era journey along the route, we depart one of the bay platforms at the south end of Preston and travel via the Preston Extension, crossing the river on the viaduct. After passing the all-timber Whitehouse North Junction signalbox on the left, our train veers right and curves away to the west on a 22ft high embankment. A girder bridge takes us over a farm track before we join the spur curving in from the south at Whitehouse West Junction. The signalbox here is also on our left, and is an attractive composite structure with timber upperworks on a brick base. Though long since demolished, the remains of the 'box are clearly visible today.

Beyond Whitehouse West, the railway immediately passes beneath the six tracks of the West Coast Main Line, emerging on the other side between open land to the south and the backs of the houses on Margaret Road to the north. To our left, the rear aspect of the short row of terraces on Buller Avenue announce the impending crossing of the busy Leyland Road, which is accomplished on a steel girder bridge emblazoned with a sign-written advertisement for the car showroom Jaguar House. This bridge was demolished soon after the line's closure and the piers removed following an accident where a woman and child were crushed against the structure after a lorry shed its load. The section of trackbed between the Preston Extension and Leyland Road has today been transformed into a 'greenway' - a misnomer if ever there was one, as the once grassy trackbed has recently been covered with a thick layer of asphalt, upon which cyclists and dog walkers swarm on fine days.

A short section of embankment takes our train alongside Penwortham Fire Station before another bridge carries the line over Stricklands Lane. This was the site of Middleforth Junction, though by the 1950s the former spur from this point to Fishergate Hill was so overgrown it was unrecognisable. We immediately curve away to the south east to join the original West Lancashire line at Penwortham Junction, at which point the line from Fishergate Hill goods station joins. The goods line was eventually singled and the signalbox here was demolished in 1961, being replaced by a ground frame. A brick arch bridge carries Hill Road above the line as we enter a cutting and climb the gentle grade, with a further occupation bridge before we enter the outskirts of Penwortham and pass beneath Cop Lane, pausing at the quaint wooden halt of the same name. Starting away again, we climb for a short distance before crossing Broad Oak Lane on the level. The stretch of trackbed between Hill Road and Broad Oak Lane has today been obliterated by Golden Way, which was constructed as part of the proposed Penwortham Bypass - a road that is unlikely ever to be completed.

*Back Lane Crossing is one of the parts of the former WLR that have been obliterated by the Penwortham Bypass. As its name implied, it was situated on a minor road a few hundred yards to the south of Penwortham Cop Lane Station, which can be seen in the background in this 28 August 1964 view. One home signal for each direction protected the crossing, and these were controlled by a lever frame located in the crossing keeper's hut; the gates, however, were operated by hand.* **Alan Castle.**

Beyond Broad Oak Lane, a farm crossing and footpath are traversed before we encounter Lindle Lane level crossing. The trackbed between the roundabout at Golden Way (which has obliterated the farm and crossing mentioned previously) and Lindle Lane survives as an unofficial footpath, and the iron bases of the signals protecting the crossing can still clearly be seen. After Lindle Lane the line continues through open fields, curving gently to the west on a shallow embankment that survives intact today. We are now approaching New Longton & Hutton station; the platforms were built on a slight curve, and unlike Cop Lane were constructed of blue brick; although as a later addition to the line, the station was equipped with timber buildings rather than the more substantial brick structures at nearby Longton Bridge and Hesketh Bank. Today the village of New Longton has grown beyond all recognition, and though the trackbed immediately adjacent to the station has been encroached upon by a number of houses, much of it is still traceable within the gardens of some properties. The station stood immediately to the west of the level crossing on Station Road but has now been completely demolished; the crossing keeper's cottage survives today, albeit much-altered, as a private dwelling.

Having departed New Longton & Hutton across Station Road, the line curves gently ever westwards as far as Nursery Lane level crossing, after which point the line straightens out. We then pass beneath Moss Lane overbridge and cross Brownhill Lane on the level, shortly afterwards plunging beneath the A59 Longton Bypass. This part of the trackbed has been utilised to carry a link road connecting the two halves of Chapel Lane under the bypass, though much of the remaining route survives as open land or taken over by the gardens of properties. Beyond the Longton Bypass, our train continues westwards through open fields until we reach Longton Bridge station. This was constructed on a curve to the eastern side of Liverpool Old Road, and was accessed by a ramp up from the road. It had a goods yard and sidings to serve the adjacent brickworks (today part of Longton Brickcroft Nature Reserve). Station buildings were provided in the typical red and yellow brick style of the WLR, while the platforms were of blue brick with timber extensions, and these continued along the bridge over Liverpool Old Road. Today, the bridge has gone and the station site has been obliterated by a small housing development.

**Above:** *Situated mid-way between Penwortham Cop Lane and New Longton & Hutton stations, Lindle Lane is a minor road providing access to local farms and the nearby Lancashire Police HQ at Hutton. Stanier 2-6-4 tank 42465 is seen approaching with the 09:13 Southport to Preston service on 21 August 1964. The signal box at New Longton & Hutton is just discernible in the far distance.* **Alan Castle.**

**Below:** *The site of Lindle Lane crossing viewed from the road in 2012; the railway crossed at an angle, as indicated by the two field gates visible here. The only clue that a railway ever passed by is the slight hump in the road, however it is possible to walk on the trackbed to the north, where a number of railway relics survive in the undergrowth.* **Author.**

*The evening shadows lengthen at the end of yet another balmy summer's day as Bolton shed's Stanier 2-6-4T 42626 rolls over the level crossing and into New Longton & Hutton with a 3-coach set forming the 19:05 Preston to Southport service on 1 September 1964. The station here differed from the others on the line, having been a late addition by the West Lancashire Railway in 1889 when the company was still experiencing financial difficulties.* **Alan Castle.**

Beyond Longton Bridge, the line curves gently, straightening out after crossing Hall Lane by means of an underbridge to head almost due southwest through virgin farmland. Another bridge carries us over Hall Carr Lane; after crossing a few more fields we cross Station Road at a level crossing and arrive at Hoole station. Despite being some considerable distance from a centre of population, passenger provision at Hoole was good. On the up (Southport-bound) platform, a long single-storey flat-roofed building contained a waiting room, toilets and a ticket office. On the opposite platform, a smaller flat-roofed structure contained a ladies' room, lamp room and an open-fronted waiting area. Behind the up platform was a siding, accessible from the Southport direction, with capacity for some 25 wagons. Due to its remote location, Hoole's platforms survive remarkably intact, albeit very overgrown. Until recently, the building on the down side also remained in situ, though this has now been demolished by the landowner. Three of the four level crossing gates can also be seen, though these are now in very poor condition.

Departing Hoole, the line continues through the unspoiled marshy landscape and begins curving once more to the west as it enters the valley of the River Douglas. A little over a mile from Hoole, we are heading almost due west as we cross the river on the impressive swing bridge, which by now had been fastened shut since the Douglas was no longer navigable for large craft. While the bridge has today been completely removed, the pier on the eastern side of the river can still clearly be seen. A short goods branch to Tarleton, opened in 1880, diverged here to serve a wharf on the Tarleton branch of the Leeds & Liverpool Canal. A railmotor passenger service was trialled on the line in 1912, but it was not a success and was withdrawn after a period of little more than a year. The entire branch fell into disuse in 1925, and was formally closed in November 1930.

Immediately after crossing the Douglas, our train approaches Hesketh Bank, and we pass the sidings serving Alty's brickworks. After passing beneath Station Road, we pause at Hesketh Bank station. The main buildings were situated on the down side, and were accessed by an approach road from the north side of the overbridge. They followed the pattern of the facilities provided at the larger WLR stations, being single-storey red and yellow brick structures with arched windows and a sloping roof. A small canopy existed at one time, though this had disappeared by the 1950s. On the up side platform, a flat-roofed waiting room similar to that at Hoole was provided; reflecting the higher status of Hesketh Bank, however, it was fully-enclosed with large glazed windows and wooden panelling. The station site has now been obliterated by a small housing estate, though the trackbed beyond remains intact.

*The crossing keeper's cottage at New Longton & Hutton survives today, albeit substantially altered, as a private dwelling. The railway line ran through the hedgeline in the foreground.* **Author.**

Continuing our journey to Southport, our train curves once more to the south west as the line crosses the marshy Hesketh Moss. The fertile growing land can clearly be seen from the low embankment, and fields of fruit and vegetables abound. A large number of enormous glasshouses are dotted around the landscape as we approach the next level crossing adjacent to the tiny station at Hundred End, just under two miles west of Hesketh Bank. Passenger facilities here consisted of a booking office, located across the road from the platforms, and a small wooden waiting hut on each platform. The platforms themselves were built of ash and cinders and faced with timber sections. While the station was small, it most certainly was not an unstaffed halt - even in the late 1950s, staff were provided in the form of two porters-cum-booking clerks. This was certainly a case of over-provision, as by this time only around 10 passengers per day used the station and the corresponding daily takings of around £1 would barely cover the staff wages! The goods yard, consisting of two sidings, officially closed in June 1957 and the station finally followed on 30 April 1962. The signalbox remained open to cater for the passage of road vehicles used by the village's 300 or so inhabitants until the closure of the line. The station site is now occupied by a private dwelling, though the remainder of the land is made up of open fields.

After passing through Hundred End, another half-dozen or so fields are crossed before the single track Gorsey Lane appears on the right. The trackbed is drained by a substantial ditch on the left-hand side, and this has prevented it becoming waterlogged even after closure. As the road curves away to our right, we approach the level crossings at Square House Lane and Long Lane to enter the outskirts of the village of Banks. The station is reached next, a little under two miles from Hundred End, and is situated to the east of Guinea Hall Lane level crossing. The buildings on the down side were almost identical to those at Hesketh Bank, with the exception that the small canopy over the waiting room door survived until the closure of the station. A two-storey house for the station master was added between the road and the station buildings in 1899. A couple of timber buildings were located next to these, along with a brick-built lamp room. On the up side was a small timber waiting shelter, and the station's signalbox was built on the western end of the platform, immediately by the ramp. The whole of the trackbed from Hundred End to Banks survives intact today, as does the station's down platform. The up platform was removed when the adjacent drainage ditch was enlarged to facilitate the construction of a housing estate on the nearby land.

Departing Banks across Guinea Hall Lane level crossing, we travel through a handful of fields before passing beneath the A565 Southport New Road. Beyond this, the line crosses the two large parallel man-made drainage channels known as The Sluice and Back Drain by means of a pair of girder bridges. Continuing to the end of the marshes on a low embankment, crossing New Lane by means of a level crossing and rumbling across the bridge over the Three Pools Waterway, the ground levels out as we enter the Southport suburbs at Crossens, reaching the station which is located on the eastern side of Bankfield Lane overbridge.

**Above:** *After leaving New Lonton & Hutton and going over the level crossings at Station Road and Nursery Lane, the line passed beneath Moss Lane bridge. Seen from Moss Lane itself, Fairburn 2-6-4 tank 42292 heads for Southport with a train from Preston on 2 March 1963. Visible in the background is the bridge beneath the A59 Longton Bypass.*

**Below:** *Another view of the RCTS 'Ribble Lune Railtour', previously seen from the train itself approaching Whitehouse West Junction. 72007* Clan Mackenzie *is heading for Southport and has just passed beneath Moss Lane bridge; the vantage point for this picture is the embankment below the A59 bridge.* **Both: Peter Fitton.**

*While the bridge beneath the A59 Longton Bypass survives intact today, the route of the former railway is now utilised by a link road that enables traffic using Chapel Lane to avoid crossing the dual carriageway on the level.* **Author.**

The crossover immediately east of Crossens station is the first place we encounter the electrified third rail, which will be alongside the running rails for the remainder of our journey to Southport. Again, the buildings on the down platform are identical to those at Banks and Hesketh Bank, while a brick-built flat-roofed waiting shelter stands on the up platform. Due to the electrified line, passengers have to cross between platforms using a footbridge, though a barrow crossing is provided for use by luggage porters. Today, sadly all traces of Crossens station have vanished; in the late 1960s an industrial estate was built, though the trackbed was left clear, although this has now been replaced by a housing estate that has obliterated the alignment completely.

Continuing from Crossens, we pass beneath Bankfield Lane and skirt between two 1940s-built housing estates before climbing above the surrounding land on an embankment. We pass close by the Botanic Gardens until, just under three-quarters of a mile from Crossens, we reach Churchtown station, located on the embankment and underbridge above Manor Road. Unusually, the booking office here is at street level on the east side of the road, there being no space on the embankment for conventional structures. Instead, the platforms are built from timber and are adorned with small wooden waiting shelters; primitive compared with the facilities at Crossens but infinitely better than today's provision for bus passengers on Manor Road! Following closure of the line, the embankment and bridge here were removed and the road level raised. A health centre now occupies the site of the former station.

Now firmly in the Southport suburbs, we continue south westwards between the gardens of Beresford Drive, Cambridge Road and Silverthorne Drive. After passing beneath the overbridge carrying Hesketh Drive, the line curves sharply southwards and we approach Hesketh Park station. The goods yard here is to the west of the line and consists of a pair of sidings with a capacity of 29 wagons; a pair of points gives access from the Preston direction. After passing these, the small but attractive signalbox can be seen to our right before the station itself comes into view. Situated on a curve, the platforms are of brick and the buildings follow the arrangement of facilities at Crossens, with the traditional WLR main buildings on the down platform and a flat-roofed brick-built waiting shelter on the up platform. The station was equipped with concrete lamp columns and electric light, together with the BR enamel 'sausage' totem signs applied to all stations from Banks westwards. As at Crossens, a footbridge provided passengers with cross-platform access. Today, most traces of Hesketh Park are gone, vanished beneath the ever-spreading housing, but on a former railway footpath that once linked the station with Henley Drive, a single concrete lamp survives as a reminder of the quaint country-style station that once existed in the heart of the Southport suburbs. Beyond Hesketh Park lies Roe Lane Junction, where the WLR forked to join the lines to Southport and Wigan, and is where we leave the journey as we pass outside the Preston area.

**Above:** *Once a common sight, but by 1964 a very rare visitor to the Southport line, is one of the last Fowler 2-6-4 Class 4 tanks, 42369, seen here making a very rousing departure from Longton Bridge on 5 September 1964 at the head of the 12:18 Saturdays only Southport to Preston. Since the closure of the goods yard here in April of that year, the signalbox was normally 'switched out' on weekends, as is the case here.* **Alan Castle.**

**Below:** *The site of Longton Bridge station viewed from street level in 2012. The bridge deck has now gone, along with most of the pier on the Preston side (to the right) where a housing estate now stands. The trackbed on the Southport side, however, survives intact as far as the River Douglas.* **Author.**

**Above:** *A very rare visitor to the line, indeed the first of its class to have been seen in over 12 months, is Stanier 'Jubilee' 45642 Boscawen, photographed leaving the lonely windswept outpost of the South Lancashire mosslands at Hoole on 5 September 1964 at the head of the 13:17 Southport to Preston 'stopper'.* **Alan Castle.**

**Below:** *The scene at Hoole station today, looking towards Preston. Both platforms survive, albeit covered in grass and weeds, and three of the four level crossing gates remain in situ beneath the overgrowth. The pile of bricks visible is all that remains of the recently-demolished waiting shelter on the down platform.* **Author.**

**Above:** *A passenger's eye view of Hesketh Bank station from the approaching 13:16 Preston to Southport on 16 August 1964. Today, the bridge carrying the road above the photographer is the only sign that a railway ever ran here, as the station site has been swallowed up by a housing estate. Fortunately, steam survives at Hesketh Bank in the shape of the narrow-gauge West Lancashire Light Railway, which runs for a short distance around the former clay pits of Alty's brickworks.*

**Below:** *The fireman of Stanier 2-6-4 tank 42484 temporarily ceases in his labours to view the derelict and overgrown timber and ash platforms of the former Hundred End station, as the 10:12 Preston to Southport service sweeps through on 16 August 1964. The station had closed to passengers two years previously.* **Both: Alan Castle.**

**Above:** *A view rearwards from the footplate of Lostock Hall's BR Standard 2MT 2-6-0 No. 78041, taking in the expanse of the down platform on the last day of the West Lancashire line at Banks on 6 September 1964, while awaiting departure time with the 14:10 working from Southport to Preston.*

**Below:** *Stanier 2-6-4 tank. 42555 accelerates its train away from the rain-sodden platforms of Hesketh Park with the 16:14 Southport to Preston on 5 September 1964. Evidence can be seen, in the form of the open doors of the goods shed to the left of the down platform, that the depot and coal yard remain very much in business, and would do so until 1967.* **Both: Alan Castle.**

**Above:** *No tour of the Preston area would be complete without taking a look at the sheds and stabling points in the area. On 27 July 1968, with just a few days to go before steam ended on British Railways, this was the scene from the top of the coaling plant at Lostock Hall. The water tank building is in the immediate foreground, with the ash plant beyond. A number of Stanier 8Fs and 'Black 5s' await their turn of duty alongside a specially 'bulled up' Riddles 'Britannia' pacific, 70013 Oliver Cromwell. Alongside are the replacement diesels in the shape of Class 25s, Class 40s and a solitary Class 50.* **Tony Gillett.**

**Below:** *Lostock Hall was never home to any premier West Coast Main Line motive power; indeed, it was mainly responsible for freight locomotives and tank engines until Preston shed burned down in June 1960. Thereafter its allocation increased, especially once Preston shed closed completely on 10 September 1961. From that point on, it occasionally played host to some glamorous visitors, as seen here on 15 February 1964 as 'Duchess' 46238 City of Carlisle is coaled before returning north, having arrived with a football special from its namesake city.* **Peter Fitton.**

**Above:** *While Lostock Hall never had an allocation of Stanier 3-cylinder 'Jubilee' 4-6-0s, they were regular visitors as they often worked in at the head of holiday excursion trains. However, the pristine condition of 45590* Travancore, *together with the lack of a shedplate on the smokebox door, in this view dating from 8 May 1962, suggests that it is more likely on running in duties after overhaul at Crewe.* **Tony Gillett.**

**Below:** *More usual motive power in this view of Lostock Hall on 26 November 1967, with Ivatt Class 4 'Flying Pig' 2-6-0 43088 alongside Stanier 8F 2-8-0 48445 hissing gently in the yard, while an unidentified Class 40 waits in front of the shed.* **Peter Fitton.**

**Above:** *Even after the June 1960 fire that destroyed the roof, Preston shed was still a hive of activity for a time. Visible in this 1 July 1961 view of the western side of the yard are the ash plant and coaling tower, while part of the shed can be seen to the right. The three locomotives were all examples of types common to the shed, and include Hughes/Fowler 'Crab' 2-6-0 42715, an impressively clean Stanier 'Black 5' 44907 and rebuilt 'Royal Scot' 46168* The Girl Guide.

**Below:** *The damage to Preston shed can clearly be seen as Stanier's first pacific, 46200* The Princess Royal, *simmers gently against the glow of the evening sun on 22 August 1961. The shed closed less han a month later.* **Both: Tony Gillett.**

**Above:** *With the end of steam in 1968, Lostock Hall shed closed and Preston once more gained a stabling point for its locomotives. This was on the site of the former Dock Street coal yard, and quite a few examples of Classes 40 and 47 can be seen in this 7 September 1978 view. In the foreground, doing its best to impersonate a steam locomotive, 47 048 has its train heating boiler tested.* **Dave Felton / Adrian Bradshaw collection.**

**Below:** *A handful of sidings were also available in the former North Union yard to the southwest of the station; the conveyor bridge visible crossing the line here carried post and parcels from the south end of platforms 3 and 4 (originally 5 and 6) to the Royal Mail sorting offices. APT-P unit 370 004 has been dragged to Preston and unceremoniously dumped in the yard after having failed during a test run. The APT sets were at their least reliable at this time, and this sight was not uncommon.* **Dave Felton**